TOMBSTONE

TOMB-STONE

By William Hattich

Foreword by

John D. Gilchriese

UNIVERSITY OF OKLAHOMA PRESS

Library of Congress Cataloging in Publication Data

Hattich, William.
  Tombstone, in history, romance and wealth.

  Reprint. Originally published: Tombstone, Ariz.: Daily Prospector,
1903.
  Includes index.
  1. Tombstone (Ariz.)—History. I. Title.
F819.T6H325 1981   979.1'53   80–5947
ISBN 0–8061–1753–2   AACR2

FOREWORD

Tombstone, Arizona, ever synonymous with the so-called "Wild West," has captivated the imagination of millions. Its very name suggests such people as Wyatt, Virgil, and Morgan Earp, Doc Holliday, Sheriff John Behan, the Clantons and McLaurys, and Johnny Ringo.

Popular and escapist literature has unfortunately relegated Tombstone's historic past to a few moments of sanguinary action in a place called the O.K. Corral. To Tombstone's long-time residents the most important event was the arrival of the railroad that would at long last connect it with the outside world.

To commemorate this event the editor of the Tombstone *Daily Prospector,* the late William Hattich, conceived this tribute to the spirit and people of Tombstone. This commemorative Tombstone imprint has for nearly eighty years remained an elusive rarity.

With the arrival in March, 1903, of the railroad Tombstone looked forward to a resurgence of its once vital role as the most important city in the Arizona Territory. At the very time the railroad arrived mining capitalists were determined to reopen Tombstone's storied silver mines and reclaim another fortune they believed waited in the subterranean depths surrounding the town.

The original publisher of this book, William Hattich, known affectionately to thousands of Arizonans as "Will," told me before his death that he published this book to focus attention on the real Tombstone and its hope for the future. Hattich arrived in Tombstone in January, 1881, joining his father who previously had established himself there as a tailor. From January, 1881, until the late summer of 1913, Hattich witnessed Tombstone's violence, growth, sudden decline, and hoped-for renaissance.

This slender tribute to Tombstone and its people offers the reader a glimpse of reality and a proper sense of proportion in lieu of garbled fiction and senseless violence.

John D. Gilchriese

CONTENTS

TOMBSTONE DAILY PROSPECTOR

TOMBSTONE, ARIZONA

TOMBSTONE

IN HISTORY, ROMANCE AND WEALTH

Souvenir Illustrated Edition, Commemorating Arrival of
Railroad to Tombstone, Arizona

PUBLISHED BY
DAILY PROSPECTOR, TOMBSTONE, ARIZONA
APRIL, 1903

A TYPICAL VIEW OF THE BIG WAGON TRAINS TO HAUL ORE FROM THE MINES BEFORE THE ADVENT OF THE RAILROAD.

PROEM

This volume is offered to the public in a spirit of sincerity. In its review of Tombstone's history, resume of its resources and forecast of its future it has carefully avoided exaggeration. Moreover, this City needs no exaggeration (assuming that any city does); its revealed resources are such that men prominent in the world of mines have left successful enter-prises of magnitude to assume its management, and one of the world's most powerful syndicates holds its Tombstone property to be the most important of its many interests. In these pages no special mention has been made of the many turbulent incidents of this City's past; for while essentially historical and inseparable from the early development of any frontier community, their violent record is better forgotten. Their inaptness to a work commemorative of industry and progress is obvious. Tombstone is on the threshold of a prosperous day, and before the Tombstone of the past shall have slipped into the blackness of the "Backward and Abysm" of time, it is well to take a last look backward that in the sunny future we may recall those stout-hearted old pioneers whose love for the once matchless mining city they had carved out of the very heart of Apache Land, caused them to fight grimly for its life during the desolate years of depression when well nigh all of its once mighty hosts had deserted it.

If this little volume shall effect in any degree perpetuation of the memory of those hearts of oak its mission shall have been justified, and its publisher will feel that its issuance was not futile, therefore this volume on Tombstone's history, its turbulent past and vista of a glorious future, is respectfully submitted.

TOMBSTONE'S DISCOVERER

 Ed. Schieffelin's Daring Exploration of Apache Land, and His Golden Reward. Brief Sketch of an Intrepid Pioneer Whose Courage Made Possible the Subsequent Development of this Famous Mining Region

WHEN Ed. Schieffelin grasped the iron hand of Fate that far day in '78 and staked his life against a problematical chance in the Apache-infested foothills of the Mules, he was already a seasoned veteran in that indomitable army of prospectors who ever lead the way into silent regions. Immutable is that army as the desolate Utgard for the feet of the oncoming civilization. The prospector is a living allegory of patience. Toiling always outward through the trackless desert, lonesome and grim, steel-thewed and untiring as the silent little burro beside him, he is the mightiest explorer and civilizer of modern times. And the "Hassayamper" is

EDWARD SCHIEFFELIN,   *Fly, Photo.*
DISCOVERER OF TOMBSTONE, AND HIS GRANITE TOMB, MARKING THE FIRST
CAMPING PLACE OF THE INTREPID PIONEER.

sun. Ever marching forward, with brave faces always set against the great unknown. No desertions ever thin their iron ranks, no complainings ever pass their lips. Their pause at each conquest is but a bivouac, for victories are but incidents in their irresistible advance. The great host of progress swells behind them and ever calls on them to conquer new lands and build trails into the perhaps the most indurated of all prospectors. It is said that the leg bones of the desert mustang, instead of being porous like those of other horses, are smooth and hard as metal. They have actually become ivory from a few generations of adaptation to the hard conditions of the waterless deserts and prairies of the Southwest. Undoubtedly, close investigation of the southern prospector would reveal somewhat similar physical changes induced by his unusual life. He has become a distinct physical class from his fellow men. With only the average man's powers of endurance, the prospector must indubitably have failed in his Tantalus task of mapping out the eerie wastes of Arizona.

Edward Schieffelin was born in Western Pennsylvania in 1848, but when he was only ten years old his father trekked westward into Oregon. With pioneer stamina as an inheritance, young Schieffelin manifested a desire to prospect as a mere boy, the banks of the Rouge river being his first field. At the age of twenty-two he had worked his way well southward and was earning a livelihood on the great Comstock lode. With more space at command, it would be interesting to follow the virile, sun-tanned young Schieffelin in his tortuous windings through the sagebrush flats of Nevada and rugged crags of Northern Arizona. Equipped with his dearly-bought and well-learned knowledge of the craft of miner and prospector,

the promising mineral aspect of the district, but it is improbable that any of them, brave men though they were, had the hardihood to risk their lives so wantonly. His perilous venture was rewarded by a discovery of great richness. He "staked it off," and, with the spirit of grim humor, gave it the name of Tombstone. Then, taking with him a few samples of the ore, he crept out of the haunt of the red men as warily as he had entered, and made his way northward to Globe. His brother Albert and Assayer Richard Gird joined him, and, returning to the claim, they began the work that soon made Tombstone famous in the annals of mining. Later they sold their interests in Tombstone and Ed. Schieffelin, although now rich, again assumed the life of prospector, penetrating to the uttermost confines of frozen Alaska. He came to his death in a lonely cabin in the heart of Oregon, dying as a prospector lives, alone, and could we view that last grim trip into the land beyond the black mountain range of Death we no doubt would see Ed. Schieffelin facing the

VIEW OF A TOMBSTONE BUSINESS THOROUGHFARE.

he began his slow advance into the unknown portion of little-known Arizona. With his pick, canteen and blankets packed on his faithful little burro, the clear southern sky his only roof, the coyote and the desert owl for cronies, and the eternal .45-60 caliber bean for diet, he continued steadily in his search for the mine he was sure sooner or later to discover. His progress was much retarded by frequent necessity of hammering a drill for a few months in some other man's mine, that he might replenish his grub supply and renew his outfit, but eventually he reached the region that was to be the scene of his future success. The manner of his entrance into the death-shadowed pass between the Mule mountains and Cochise's stronghold is eloquent testimony of the man's clear strain courage. He came southward from Wickenburg with a party of Indian scouts, themselves on the very trail of the red-handed hostiles; yet, when the party had reached San Pedro, Schieffelin left them and advanced alone into the inner fastness of the murderous savages. There may have been many other prospectors aware of

king of terrors with eye as steady and heart as tranquil as when he came into the Valley of the Red Death twenty years before. His body has been brought back from the chill North, even as he wished, to rest forever on the granite hill where he kept sleepless vigil that first night before he entered the valley that held out equal chance of horrid death or golden fortune. The simple inscription on the monument built to his memory is significant of the intrepid pioneer's life:

EDWARD SCHIEFFELIN.

———

DIED MAY 12, 1897.

———

Aged 49 Years, 8 Months.

———

A DUTIFUL SON.
A FAITHFUL HUSBAND.
A KIND BROTHER.
A TRUE FRIEND.

Tombstone, Old and New

The Southwest's Peerless Metropolis of the '80's; Its Romantic History, Past Glories, Reminiscences and Future Rehabilitation

TOMBSTONE, from a historic view point, may be regarded as an anti-climax. The El Dorado of California, the seething tide of human progress that reached its flood at the Golden Gate in the "days of '49" was the culminating epoch in the Saga of the fair-skinned race who started upon their irresistible way eons agone from Hindu Kuh's jungled base in the black bole of the mystic East. Checked in their westward march by the broad Pacific, seeing their host subsiding into the placid ways of those who have reached the goal, the more venturesome spirits, like warrior veterans who can not brook a life of peace, set their faces to the southward, and once more built an industrial monument to the vigor of their kind in the sun-scalded hills and desert reaches of Arizona. Tombstone, in the days of the Southland's grandeur, was

felin, who outdid in daring all his iron-ribbed comrades. Penetrating with the wariness of the desert-bred to the very heart of the cruel hostile's ground—home of the red death—he placed his white man's brand upon the spot, and, with a fearless man's grim humor, named it—Tombstone.

With the news of Schieffelin's "find," too marvelously rich to need exaggeration for the most exacting visionary, began a mining excitement and a concomitant rush such as has seldom been surpased in the history of the United States. Lured by the story of treasure came a pioneer host, drawn from every corner of the civilized world. Suntanned veterans of the plains, alert denizens of the city, laborers, mechanics, men dexterous in the arts, Teuton, Celt and Latin, came racing southward toward the border to build, between the Mule and Dragoon mountains, one

CITY OF TOMBSTONE.

its proud metropolis; for this sentient community, on the border of white man's civilization, has writ its story in flaming letters upon the scroll of American history. It has been the most vivid splotch of color on the horizon of the West, one of the grandest cantos in the Gringo's Iliad.

Tombstone, born of the glamour and magic of weird Apache Land, for more than a generation has been the Avatar of all that romance has woven of the great American Southwest—the lorn coyote's sage brush realm, whose mystic spell has held more of subtle allurement than ever the dim vistas of the antique orient. The venturesome Argonauts of this age who held their intrepid way across a trackless continent, or rounded the horn, 'mid perils of a sunless sea, to make an Aryan empire upon the Pacific, and again gave their sturdiest man, still undaunted, to the conquest of this far land of soul-withering desolation and lurking death, sent with those wire-thewed, keen-eyed outriders of civilization's advance, lion-hearted old Ed. Schief-

of the most vigorous and cosmopolitan communities the Occident has ever held. Uncouth hoists upreared their grim hulks upon the sky-line, shafts and tunnels crept unceasingly into the world-old treasure hoards of the hills, roads were cut athwart the prairie, and the busy men builded homes and business houses until, within a brief span of months, what had been a bleak, untrod plateau, was a city of broad streets, flanked with substantial buildings and teeming with a virile, hustling swarm of humanity. Like all frontier communities that have flashed into being, isolate from the concrete bulk of their civilization, Tombstone, in the beginning, was tough. The swash-buckler with his educated gun was here in abundance, and that he saved the early settler from any languor of spirits goes without saying. In his strenuous endeavors to banish the ennui induced by a tame existence of whisky drinking and faro, he often accomplished much good and enthusiastic shooting, and, so long as he confined his brawls to his own ranks, he was allowed to pursue the even tenor of his way unmolested. But the bad man is merely a symptom—the measles period, so to speak —of a mining camp's adolescence; and when the busy

were thronged with the same motley crowd of racial opposites; she was the same breeding place of the reckless spirit that has made of the United States a new and

COUNTY HOSPITAL.   PUBLIC SCHOOL BUILDING.
PUBLIC BUILDINGS IN TOMBSTONE.
CITY HALL.   COURT HOUSE.

yeomanry of Tombstone became tired of his pyrotechnic spree they made him evanesce. To attempt even a resume of the more salient features of Tombstone's lurid past would require a volume, and is, of course, not within

greater Rome. The picturesque stage coach, with its dexterous driver and mettlesome horses, that inspired much of Bret Harte's romance, was Tombstone's only medium of communication with the outside world. Harte's very

TOMBSTONE'S FAMOUS STAGE.
PASSING OF THE HISTORIC CONCORD STAGE WHICH HAS SEEN MUCH SERVICE AND MANY THRILLING EXPERIENCES.

the province of a brief article. She was much like her prototype on San Francisco Bay—a renaissance of the golden days of the early '50's on the Coast. Her streets

Yuba Bill may have held the ribbons once again between here and Benson or Bisbee. And those stage drivers had more than one brush with the enterprising highwayman on their way to and from the Southwestern metropolis. The freighters, too, were as hardy and picturesque a craft as ever trod the earth; gaunt, eagle-eyed "skinners," ever alert for the treacherous Apache as they urged onward with volleying profanity, their magnificent mules, twenty-two in a team, tall, clean limbed, presenting a magnificent spectacle as they drew their towering "prairie schooners" onward through the glinting sunlight. Oxen were used to haul the heavier freight of lumber and machinery. Slow they were, to be sure; but their great strength, in its tireless advance, was as irresistible as the ocean's tide.

The freighting stage coach phase is a community's most spectacular period, but it makes necessaries assume extravagant prices. In those early days such homely household attributes as butter and sugar assumed a worth that placed them among the sybaritic luxuries, while a pair of good boots were worth as much as a good horse. Yet, with all adverse conditions, the richness of the mines built

water, the two mines referred to were obliged perforce to lower the flow in all the neighboring shafts. The owners of the latter unjustly refused to contribute their share of the great expense involved, with the inevitable result that work ceased. Tombstone's palmy days faded as rapidly as they had come. Business steadily lagged, the hum of industry ceased, and what had been a city of ten thousand souls shrank into a desolate, half-hearted village, whose population could be measured by three figures. For many years the once peerless mining camp of the Southland has dwelt in the shadow of doubt, to the outside world seemingly forsaken forever by the host of industry and progress; but a few staunch pioneer spirits of her days of pride, ever daunted by oft-deferred hope, are at last realizing that their unfaltering trust in the old camp is to be justified. The man who has known success as a miner beyond any in Arizona; who, by reason of his prominent identification in the past with Tombstone mines, should know more

EPISCOPAL CHURCH.   CATHOLIC CHURCH.   METHODIST CHURCH.

Tombstone steadily larger, and continued paying princely dividends until the little desert city became known and famed the wide world over. Its prosperity built tributary towns, it formed a base for exploration of a hitherto inaccessible region; ranchers settled along the San Pedro river, and, as their trade increased with Tombstone's upbuilding, thousands of cattle were shipped into the San Pedro and Sulphur Springs valleys, transforming them into one of the greatest cattle ranges in the Union. And the mines continued in richness and ever increased their output until the first ten years of the camp's existence had measured a yield of $30,000,000.00. But the pendulum that had swung so far outward into the golden years of prosperity one day ceased and then more rapidly returned. Two mines—the Grand Central and the Contention—had installed monster pumps on their properties. The entire group of mines of the district were flooded by what was practically an under-ground lake, and, in freeing their own workings of

than any other of the source of her one-time prosperity—this man has returned, with a colossal syndicate at his command, to bring to the surface the treasure that still lies beneath Tombstone's hills. Modern machinery, beside which the ponderous pumps of the '80's seem futile toys, are hurling a river of water to the surface; a shaft larger than any ever before sunk this side of mighty Butte is steadily making its way into the earth; new buildings are springing up, old ones being rehabilitated; the once mighty camp of the years gone by is waking and growing into the mightier camp of the years to be. She is not flaring upward with the feverish haste that characterized her birth—the difficulties to be overcome are Titanic and can not be brushed aside in a day; but the water flows outward in a steady river to join the San Pedro, the ore bodies are slowly and surely being uncovered; already the railroad is here to carry away the treasure that once more shall make a factor in the mining world the historic city of Tombstone.

THE RAILROAD

Tombstone Connected With the Outside World and on Line of Trans-Continental Highway

THE opening of the railroad era of a country and that of its mining field are always coincident. No mining region, however rich, may reach its full development without the aid of the iron horse of commerce. Not only do rich properties pay greater dividends when in touch with the steel roadway, but properties otherwise worthless become revenue yielding by its aid. Especially is this so in the Southwest, where towns are isolate from the greater bases of supply and widely separated each from the others. In the days of this city's beginning machinery and supplies were at first freighted overland from Yuma, then the Southern Pacific terminus in Arizona, the seemingly impossible distance of several hundred miles. Even well along in the eighties one had to traverse the distance be-

road that is at last here is not the least factor in the tremendous enterprise that may build in the years to be a city occupying the same relative importance to the Arizona of the future that Tombstone held in the ensemble of the Arizona gone by. As it is certain that no mining region may be thoroughly explored without the railroad's aid, also just so true is it that without the assurance of material resources to be developed the railroad will not be extended into a new tract of country. Obviously the financiers who build the roads do so with the object of personal gain. Therefore, the scream of the engine's whistle in new hills is assurance that curious man has found another of old Mother Nature's treasure hoards, and has come with his huge black horse of iron to carry

FIRST RAILROAD FOR TOMBSTONE—VIEW OF E. P. & S. W. R. R. WORK TRAIN CROSSING LINE OF CITY LIMITS,
MARCH 27, 1903.

tween Benson and Tombstone by aid of the old Concord coach; which conveyance, although picturesque in literature, must give way to the oncoming iron horse. Had Tombstone been in connection with a railroad from the beginning the possibilities of the past that might have been are too wide in scope for even imaginative speculation. What became a city of ten thousand souls might have contained fifty thousand—might even have surpassed in output of ore and municipal magnitude the historic Comstock at its golden zenith. For who knows what the development of Tombstone's mines on a scale of sufficient magnitude might not have brought forth from the earth's black bole? What might have been done, however, can be accomplished in the days to come. The mines that barely have had their backs scratched in the past are to be thoroughly explored in the near future, and the rail-

it out to the marts of the world. Tombstone needs no such assurance that treasure is in her hills. The lid was lifted and a few handfuls of the abundant store of wealth removed; so we know it is there. But the grind of the big engine's drivers on the grade, and its sullen hum as it rests on the hills, seemingly making grumbling estimate of the new task added to its labor, is cheering and satisfying because we know the time for the new beginning has come. The El Paso & Southwestern Railroad have built a branch line of nine miles from Fairbank on their system to Tombstone. The survey has been continued forty-five miles to College Peak, and with its completion Tombstone will ultimately be on the main line of a transcontinental route. March, 1903, marks the advent of the railroad to Tombstone, and will prove a prominent factor in the development of the rich resources which its lines traverse.

TOMBSTONE'S FAMOUS MINES

Largest Combination Shaft in the West—Immense Pumping Capacity for the Work of Draining
the Lower Levels—Powerful Mining Machinery—The Tombstone Consolidated Mines
Company, Limited, a Mammoth Enterprise, Whose Success Is Assured

THE Tombstone Consolidated Mines Company, a consolidation of ninety-five per cent. of the mines of Tombstone, that in the past have produced ore at a profit, is undoubtedly the greatest mining undertaking in the history of the Southwest. When abandoned in consequence of personal differences existing between the owners of the various properties, enough development work had been done in the deepest workings to demonstrate the existence of large bodies of pay ore below water level, as

prevented development of the Tombstone district. The organization of the Tombstone Consolidated Mines Company, Limited, was perfected, and so soon as contracts of purchase for the necessary properties had been obtained a large four-compartment shaft was started downward into the buttes or collection of hills that covered the ore body. The shaft, ten by twenty-four feet, located on the Flora Morrison claim of the Contention Consolidated Mining Company's group, was begun in May, 1901. It is now

STEEL-COVERED HOIST OF TOMBSTONE CONSOLIDATED MINES CO.

may be attested by the attempts since made by the owners to reopen their properties. But they seemed unable to unite in any concerted effort to rid the workings of the enormous flow of water that made the rich deposits inaccessible. The above mentioned company has adopted the only possible course of action consonant with success. To obviate the probability of any legal complications that might arise from diverse ownerships it was deemed necessary to purchase the mines required. This ownership of all the ore producing properties by one company obviously removes at the outset the obstacle that in the past has

below the seven-hundred-foot level and is going steadily downward as the water level lowers. The shaft has four compartments, two for rock and two for pumps. Its dimensions, with exception of one in Butte, Montana, are unequaled by any other shaft in the West. It measures seven by twenty-two feet inside the timbers, which are of the best quality Oregon pine, ten-by-ten-inch above, and twelve-by-twelve-inch below, the water level. Two hoisting engines have been installed. These engines are massive machines with tremendous power and reel capacity for practically unlimited depth. A double reel, first motion, flat rope, sixteen-by-sixty-inch cylinder hoist for lifting the rock, is supplemented by a smaller geared engine with sixteen-by-twenty-four-inch cylinders to handle the pumps.

capacity of the former pumping plants of the Grand Central and Contention Mining Companies. They are of the direct acting type, triple expansion, with steam cylinders

GLIMPSE OF THE INTERIOR OF HOISTING WORKS AND ONE OF THE LARGE 16x60-IN. CYLINDER HOISTS OF THE TOMBSTONE CONSOLIDATED MINES CO.

The latter have a lifting capacity of two million five hundred thousand gallons of water every twenty-four hours—five hundred thousand gallons more than the combined

in pairs, of thirty-nine-inch, twenty-three-inch, and fifteen-inch diameter. The diameter of the water plunger is thirteen inches, its stroke is twenty-four inches. These pumps

T. C. M. CO. HOIST.　　TOUGHNUT MILL.　　TOUGHNUT HOIST.　　WEST SIDE HOIST.

SOME OF THE PROPERTIES OF THE TOMBSTONE CONSOLIDATED MINES CO.

OTHER LARGE HOISTING WORKS CONTROLLED BY THE COMPANY IN THE DISTRICT INCLUDE THE TRANQUILLITY, SILVER THREAD, HEAD CENTER, EMERALD, GRAND CENTRAL, COMET, VIZNA, LUCKY CUSS, ETC.

are thirty-three feet seven and three-eighths inches in length, nine feet eight inches in breadth and more than six feet high. These powerful pumps will throw one thousand seven hundred and fifty gallons per minute. One of

by far the largest in Arizona, having a capacity for stored power that is beyond the conception of the non-scientific mind of the layman. These mammoth boilers could be transported from the railway only by means of specially

VIEW OF PUMPING STATION 600 FEET BELOW SURFACE.
ONE OF THE MAMMOTH PUMPS INSTALLED BY THE TOMBSTONE CONSOLIDATED MINES COMPANY
ON 600 FOOT LEVEL.   CAPACITY, 1,750 GALLONS PER MINUTE.

them has already been installed on the six-hundred-foot level. The others will be placed at the eight-hundred and one-thousand-foot levels, as the latter depths are reached. The sinking pumps are simple, direct acting duplex pumps with fourteen-by-twelve-inch cylinders and eight-inch plungers. Of these there are five. Three are to be in con-

constructed wagons. Their individual weight was fifty thousand pounds, the four of them aggregating the tremendous weight of one hundred tons. To guard against fire, which has proven so destructive in the past, the buildings and gallows frames have been constructed solely of steel. The plans of the company also include the construc-

A TOMBSTONE STREET SCENE.

stant use, while the fourth is lowering and the fifth held in reserve. The boiler plant consists of four 250-horse-power internal furnace boilers, made for an hundred and twenty-five pounds working pressure. These boilers are

tion of a smelter, or reduction plant, suited to the needs of the ore produced.

As the shaft has progressed the flow of water has increased, rushing inward from the sides as well as from beneath, the whole district adding pressure as the water in the big shaft sinks below the general level; but the pumps continue to handle the tumultuous under-world flood with precision and ease. At a depth of one hundred and twenty feet below water level they are sending swirling upward one million six hundred thousand gallons per

were known to exist at the time of the destructive fire in the Grand Central and Contention mines, which not only destroyed the pumping plants that were holding the water in check, but demolished the shafts and workings, making inaccessible a great portion of the ore bodies above water level. The phenomenal earnings of the mines in the past

A CORNER OF THE BIG PUMPING SHAFT OF THE TOMBSTONE CONSOLIDATED MINES CO.
VIEW ON 600-FOOT LEVEL, SHOWING SOME OF THE PIPES AND CONNECTIONS.

day, and the managers believe the full capacity of their immense water lifting machinery will never be required.

The mines have been examined and reported on by mining engineers of unquestioned ability and integrity, and their unanimous opinion is that the geological evidence and history of the mines are all in favor of continuation of the ore deposit to great depth. The expectations of the company are necessarily based on conditions as they

will doubtless be increased for various reasons. Improved methods of ore treatment necessarily must effect greater saving of values; the economical handling of the water by one organization with modern pumping machinery, and the great saving over the clumsy freighting facilities of the past by railroad transportation—all should contribute largely to greater production and profits. The company, conservative in all its statements, confidently expects when

SIDE ELEVATION OF TOMBSTONE'S FIRST RAILROAD DEPOT, E. P. & S. W. R. R.—FROM ARCHITECTURAL DRAWING.

the mines are opened in accordance with existing plans there will be realized a net dividend revenue greatly in excess of the published estimates. A condition that must have much weight in inspiring a trust in increased profits

of E. B. Gage, president of the company, a brief sketch of whose interesting career appears elsewhere in these pages, and General Manager W. S. Staunton—both successful men in the mining world, possessing the knowledge only to be

BATTERY OF ARIZONA'S LARGEST BOILERS.
FOUR BOILERS WEIGHING 25 TONS EACH AND COMBINED CAPACITY OF OVER 1,000 HORSEPOWER
FURNISH THE POWER FOR THE COLOSSAL MACHINERY AND MODERN PUMPING
PLANT OF THE TOMBSTONE CONSOLIDATED MINES CO.

In the future, is the fact that the work last done before the litigation between diverse interests and the destructive fire brought mining operations to a close, showed the ore to be increasing in gold values with greater depth.

acquired by wide experience. They have a thorough personal knowledge of the mines held by their company, Mr. Gage being formerly president and superintendent of the Grand Central Mining Company, while Mr. Staunton was

VIEW OF 30-HORSE TEAM AND SPECIALLY CONSTRUCTED WAGON TRANSPORTING ONE OF THE MAMMOTH 50,000-POUND
BOILERS OF THE TOMBSTONE CONSOLIDATED MINES CO. TO THE MINES.

Although not yet exploring for ore, the big shaft and the pumping station on the six-hundred-foot level have disclosed ore of great richness. The work of development and operation is being carried on under the supervision

superintendent of the Tombstone Mill and Mining Company's mines in the days of the camp's prosperous past. The value of the aggregate production of gold and silver from the mines of Tombstone, compiled by competent judges, partly from records and partly from estimate, is placed at not less than $34,000,000.00. Professor William P. Blake, of the University of Arizona, one of the ablest mining engineers in the West, in a paper treating of the geology and veins of Tombstone, published in 1882, is placed at $7,359,000.00. The following table from the paper shows the distribution of the output among the mines and mills prior to 1882:

Powder, now worth 15 cents per pound, at that time cost one dollar. Other supplies have decreased accordingly, and mining machinery and methods have improved so wonderfully during the last twenty years that mines considered worthless a few years ago are now paying handsome dividends. What, then, may not be expected from Tombstone's mines, with its rich and easily-reduced ores? The only added cost is that of the mighty pumps, but, when

STEEL GALLOWS FRAME ON SURFACE.
COMBINED HOISTING AND PUMPING SHAFT OF TOMBSTONE CONSOLIDATED MINES CO.
LARGEST SHAFT IN THE WEST—FOUR COMPARTMENTS AND FRAMED
TO BOTTOM WITH 12x12-INCH TIMBERS.

Tombstone Mill and Mining Co...	$2,704,936.33
Contention Consolidated	2,703,144.39
Grand Central	1,050,875.30
Head Center	191,520.52
Vizina	526,716.98
Ingersoll	15,000.00
Sunset	15,000.00
Corbin Mill	40,000.00
Boston Mill	112,000.00

When one considers that in those early days the railroad was at first over one hundred miles away, over which great distance machinery and supplies were brought by mule teams, some conception may be had of the great richness of the ore produced. Even when the railroad was brought to Fairbank, freights were still disastrously high.

considered with reference to the huge tonnage of ore production contemplated, it becomes almost a negligible factor of expense; and, once the basin of water is drained, it will be reduced to an insignificant figure. Old-time miners of the district do not hesitate even to say that they would not be surprised to see Tombstone assume the proportions of one of the foremost gold producers of the world. Although known as a silver camp, it is a fact that the ore has shown a steady increase of gold values as the mines have gone downward. Mines that carried no gold on the surface had an average gold value at the water level of $35.00, and increased until, not far below water level, the ore carried $100.00 in gold per ton. Geologists and many experts believe that this condition will continue in greater proportion hundreds of feet farther down. A mining expert of wide experience and intimate acquaintance with the past history of this camp is of the firm opinion that, under the conditions now prevailing, silver alone, even at the

transformation would meet his sight! The towering steel buildings that have replaced the wooden ones of former years, the mighty boilers throbbing beneath them, one of

ENGINE NO. 2 OF THE TOMBSTONE CONSOLIDATED MINES CO., SHOWING LARGE REEL AND INDICATOR.

present low prices of that metal, would prove more profitable than it did at its higher price twenty years ago. Considered broadly in all its bearings, there is probably no

the greatest pumping plants in America, driving to the surface a tremendous column of water equal in volume to the flow of the San Pedro river, of which it has become

RELIC OF FORMER DAYS—THE OLD GRAND CENTRAL PUMP, DESTROYED BY FIRE.

mining property in the country to-day that approaches in promise that of Tombstone.

Could Ed. Schieffelin view Tombstone to-day what a

a tributary, and a huge modern locomotive, the company's own great Mogul, rumbling round the curves of Tombstone's re-awakened hills. In the near future all of Tombstone's departed thousands will have returned, the throb of fully restored strength will once more pulse through her busy streets, and, with the hum of her industry once again swelling to its full diapason, she will continue her long checked growth until the one-time peerless city of the Southwest shall have once again become the greater metropolis of the New Arizona, and astonish the mining world with her production.

A SNAP SHOT BELOW THE WATER LEVEL.

ONE END OF THE LARGE COMBINATION SHAFT AT BOTTOM, SHOWING THE WATER STREAMING IN FROM ALL SIDES. MINERS
WEAR RUBBER SUITS AND CONTINUALLY WORK IN WATER. FOUR SINKING PUMPS ARE KEPT AT WORK AND
FIFTH HELD IN RESERVE. AT DEPTH OF 120 FEET BELOW WATER LEVEL, WHEN
VIEW WAS TAKEN, THE DAY'S PUMPING RECORD SHOWS 1,600,000
GALLONS PUMPED TO SURFACE.

TOMBSTONE PUBLIC SCHOOLS.

THE character and merits of a city may be gauged by the quality of its schools. Tombstone's public school's faculty has always been excellent, many of its past members having occupied professorships in some of the country's most prominent universities, and its general personnel has always been well above the average. The school building, which, with other public buildings of Tombstone, appears in this volume, is spacious and commodious, outfitted with all the modern improvements conducive to the health and comfort of the pupils. The school also has a large and creditable library. The present staff of teachers of the Tombstone public school are: Principal, Prof. J. N. Gaines; assistant, Jesse Simmons; grades, intermediate, Mrs. N. E. Carson; primary, Miss Jennie Boatman.

TOMBSTONE WATER SYSTEM.

TOMBSTONE'S water system is equaled by few in the West. The water furnished by the Huachuca Water Company flows through pipes from the snow-fed crystal streams of the beautiful Huachuca canyons, across the San Pedro river and valley, and up into the Tombstone hills, where it is stored above the city in an immense reservoir.

It is spring water, pure and abundant. The installation of another water system has also recently been accomplished. Recent analysis of the water pumped from the deeper levels of the mines shows it also to be organically pure. It is now being supplied to consumers in Tombstone by the Tombstone Improvement Company. Thus Tombstone is being supplied by two companies, insuring it against any possible future scarcity of water.

TOMBSTONE FIRE DEPARTMENT.

PERHAPS no community of like size on the globe can boast of a better fire system than that possessed by Tombstone. A pipe line thirty-five miles long, leading from the summit of the lofty Huachuca mountains, gives this city a supply of water with enough force to tear a hole through an ordinary building. The fire department comprises three volunteer hose companies, each having a separate building, in different parts of the city, and possessing all the adjuncts and equipment necessary to modern methods of fire fighting. The three hose companies are: Engine Company No. 1, Rescue Company No. 2, and Protection Company No. 3. J. W. Clark, an esteemed Tombstone resident, is chief of the fire department.

Prominent Mining Men
Who are Making
Arizona Famous

E. B. GAGE,
President Tombstone Consolidated Mines Co.

IN THESE piping days of peace the soldier of trade has superseded him of the sword. The saner opinion of modern times has come to see that through the builder of material progress and not through the slayer of his fellows. The selfishness that impels a man to build a fortune is the essential unit of value in human progress. To the prosperity of any community an industrial leader is as wholly essential as is the officer to his army, and invariably the industrial officer has secured his place of command through sheer ability.

Therefore the individual who builds for himself and his

E. B. GAGE.

ARIZONA'S MOST SUCCESSFUL MINING OPERATOR, WHO HAS MADE POSSIBLE
THE REHABILITATION OF TOMBSTONE.

fellows is the race to be perpetuated and made nobler. "Captain of Industry" has become an idiom of our language. And justly is it so, for the captain of industry is the leader into the way whose goal spells success alike for the individual and the commonwealth. For no man can build an industrial enterprise without benefiting his fellows within the prescribed limits of legitimate endeavor is entitled to all honor accorded him. Such a man is E. B. Gage, president of the company that is bringing Tombstone out of her obscurity to place her once more upon the height of usefulness and success. His clean and successful record as a great mining operator inspires confidence in him alike with the mining world and with Tombstone's people. His honest, legitimate toil in the world of mines has built up gigantic enterprises and made him a powerful factor in the realm of finance. Being alike a pioneer of Tombstone, and its mines being known by him intimately from their inception, ever appealing to him through that knowledge for recognition, they became to him a source of deep concern, a self-imposed duty that must be fulfilled—became, in short, his greatest motive, his life interest. When the project of consolidation of Tombstone's many mines was broached, the fact that E. B. Gage was the prime mover in the proposed venture impelled many mining magnates to become interested in the undertaking. He was president and superintendent of the Grand Central Mining company in the camp's palmy days, and the knowledge that he has never doubted the practicability of one day opening up the mines upon a grander scale than ever before has been the inspiration of the hope of all those who have retained their unfaltering trust in Tombstone's future. For he is no carpet knight in the industrial army. Possessing a complete knowledge of each phase and every detail of the art, he need trust nothing blindly to subordinates. The work of development and operation of the Tombstone Consolidated Mines Company is carried on under his direct supervision, as has been the case with the many other prominent properties he has made successful. The famous Congress gold mine, the greatest gold producer in the Southwest, is an instance of his managerial economy and ability. Beyond his mere worth as an operator and the trust inspired by his exact knowledge of the conditions and ore bodies beneath the present water level, there is a bond of sympathy between Tombstone's people and the man who has never forsaken or doubted the city's potential worth, for the great undertaking of the Tombstone Consolidated Mines Company is but the fruition of the year-long hopes and efforts of its president. Personally, also, Mr. Gage is typical of the Arizonan. Hale or body, clear of mind, strong-featured and observant, with the affable, open manner of the true Southwesterner, his nature completely fulfills the popular conception of that essentially Western character, the pioneer. Mr. Gage was born in Pelhan, New Hampshire, October 2, 1839. As a boy he attended the common school, and at the age of fifteen entered the preparatory school at Phillip's Academy, Andover, Massachusetts, going from there to Dartmouth college, where he graduated from the scientific department in 1858. In 1877 he came to Arizona and the following year became interested in the Grand Central mines. Although possessing a busy man's indifference to politics, recognition of his worth and integrity has called him at times into the public's service. He was four years a prison commissioner and was president of the capitol commission during the erection of that building. At present he is one of the board of directors of the great mining syndicate known as the Development Company of America, president of the Phœnix National Bank, president of the Congress Gold Mining Company, president of the Consolidated Tombstone Gold Mines Company and one of the directors of the Sante Fe, Prescott & Phœnix Railway. He is a man of quiet and domestic tastes and stands to-day strong in the consciousness of well-spent years devoted to a field of productive industry affording employment for an army of Arizona workers. The great success that has attended his labors as a result of untiring enterprise, remarkable ability, good judgment, liberality and public spirit, is a conspicuous and worthy example of what may be accomplished in the struggle for success in life.

F. M. MURPHY,
President Development Company of America.

ANY reference to the mining career of Mr. Gage would be incomplete without mention of Frank M. Murphy, who for years has been an able associate of the former gentleman. He was Mr. Gage's able ally in the upbuilding of the Congress mine, and although not concerned in direct management of the local company, he occupies the position of president of the parent corporation, of which the Tombstone Consolidated Mines Company is the most important division. Like Mr. Gage, Mr. Murphy is a mining pioneer of Arizona, having contributed incalculably to the territory's development. At present he is identified with many of Arizona's largest interests; most prominently as president of the Santa Fe, Prescott and Phoenix Railroad (part of the Atchison, Topeka & Santa Fe system), and president of the Prescott National Bank.

FRANK M. MURPHY.
FOREMOST AMONG THE MEN WHO HAVE MADE ARIZONA GREAT IN THE WORLD OF INDUSTRY.

Mr. Murphy is also numbered among Arizona's worthy pioneers, his residence dating back over twenty years. His forceful character, excellent judgment and energetic spirit has gained for him recognition as one of Arizona's foremost and influential citizens. The welfare of Arizona's commercial, industrial and financial interests and her mining success always finds a ready and willing encourager in Mr. Murphy, and the treasure territory is greatly indebted to him for the unfailing support he extends all projects conceived in the interest of her material welfare, and for the accomplishment of the great results that have inured to her benefit and development through his efforts. His successful financiering of mammoth Arizona enterprises has been phenomenal, and his rare business ability is recognized and conceded, while he also commands the respect and esteem of all who know him.

W. F. STAUNTON,
General Manager Tombstone Consolidated Mines Co.

W. F. STAUNTON, general manager of the Consolidated Mines Company, for many years has been Mr. Gage's able lieutenant, contributing incalculably to the success of their mining operations by his unsurpassed knowledge of the profession. He not only ranks as one of the most brilliant mining engineers and mining authorities in the West, but is invaluable to Tombstone's future development, because of the thorough knowledge of its mines and their conditions, derived from close association with their operation in the past.

Than W. F. Staunton there are few, if any, who have more thoroughly mastered the contents of the great tome of mining knowledge. Since the days when as a youth

W. F. STAUNTON,
WHOSE MINING KNOWLEDGE AND SUCCESSFUL MANAGERIAL POLICY HAS MADE HIM PRE-EMINENT AMONG ARIZONA'S MINING MEN.

he became a student of that interminable study of the world's hidden secrets, he has availed himself of every opportunity that afforded a chance for acquirement of new data or knowledge of principles of that abstruse art; and by ceaseless enthusiasm, tireless energy and a wonderfully retentive mind, he has attained a position in the mining world occupied by few mining men in the Southwest. Among others, his report on the Tombstone mines—the history of their past development, the present conditions of their ore bodies, probable manner of their future development, and the methods necessary to their proper treatment—is one of the most comprehensive and masterly papers on the subject ever submitted. He is, moreover, one of those clear-sighted managers whose wisely conservative policy has always tempered the ultra-enthusiastic animus of a new mining country, and thereby prevented the harm that is often done to undeveloped regions by the unthinking boomer. To men possessing the equable, calm judgment and resolute

integrity of such eminent mining men as W. F. Staunton and associates, Arizona owes the steady development of its greatest industry.

H. KINSLEY,
Treasurer Tombstone Consolidated Mines Co.

ANOTHER prominent citizen who has become identified with the Tombstone Consolidated Mines Company, and thereby becoming a valuable resident of Tombstone, is Mr. Kinsley, treasurer of the above mentioned company. Mr. Kinsley's intimate knowledge and thorough acquaintance with all matters pertaining to finance and positions of trust and responsibility, and his complete understanding of the requirements and duties of his office, makes him at once a valued and efficient officer. Mr. Kinsley is closely allied with the Prescott National Bank, of Prescott, Ariz., one of the leading financial institutions of the territory, and well-known in banking circles throughout the Southwest, enjoying the confidence and trust of people high in the esteem of their fellow citizens. He is known as a man of extremely quiet but pleasant demeanor, with a conservativeness and business acumen that insures the success of any undertaking which may enlist his efforts, and, from his position of cashier and director of the Prescott National Bank, he is eminently fitted for the duties of his office and the material benefaction of the interests of his company. He is an enthusiastic Arizonan, having the interests of the territory ever at heart, and reposes great faith in the future greatness and prosperity of the city which now numbers him among her progressive residents.

H. M. ROBINSON,
Secretary Tombstone Consolidated Mines Co.

INCLUDED among the roll of foremost and prominent spirits whose interests and admirable confidence in the ultimate success and return of the old-time activity of the once booming and thriving metropolis of this section of the Southwest, is to be commended, and whose ability it is to exert the influence he enjoys to the restoring of renewed actual prosperity of this famous mining camp, is Mr. H. M. Robinson, a prominent attorney of Youngstown, Ohio, secretary of the Tombstone Consolidated Mines Company, Limited.

Although Mr. Robinson is a young man, his sterling qualities have gained for him an envious reputation as a man of professional ability and business acumen, and the respect and admiration of a wide circle of friends in the industrial and financial world.

His qualities of energy and comprehensiveness have attained for him a most enviable position in financial circles, being distinguished as an organizer of not a few large and well known enterprises. Personally, Mr. Robinson enjoys great popularity among his associates, which can be attributed to his pleasing and engaging manners and generous and sympathetic disposition.

In his position of secretary of the Tombstone Consolidated Mines Company, Limited, Mr. Robinson has displayed such a practical knowledge of the actual requirements and duties attending same that would wholly warrant the confidence and trust reposed in him. His interest in Arizona was enlisted several years ago, from which time his confidence and enthusiasm in her resources has never waned.

ARTHUR N. GAGE,
Assistant Secretary and Treasurer Tombstone Consolidated Mines Co.

ARTHUR N. GAGE, assistant secretary and treasurer of the Tombstone Consolidated Mines Company, is a young man of pronounced individual energy and indefatigable worker, whose devotion to duty has made for him a proud reputation in his field of work. His executive ability and knowledge of detail acquired by experience in connection with many successful enterprises throughout the territory has eminently fitted him for his position of trust as assistant secretary and treasurer of the mammoth enterprise that has brought about a resuscitation of historic Tombstone.

Mr. Gage is closely identified with men of prominence who have asserted their faith in the glorious future of the coming Cripple Creek of the Southwest—Tombstone— and being himself a former resident of this city, he, like his associates, entertains great confidence in this section's future greatness. Mr. Gage's known ability, coupled with an admirable individuality, has entitled him to the esteem and respect of all who know him.

TOMBSTONE CHURCHES.

THERE are four churches in Tombstone, representing as many denominations and sects, and services in each are well attended. The churches and pastors are: Episcopal, Rev. Elliott, pastor; Methodist, Rev, Ramey, pastor; Catholic, Father Meurer, pastor; Congregational, Rev. Anderson. Services in the latter church are held at the city hall.

A DELIGHTFUL CLIMATE.

THE Tombstone climate is unquestionably superb, and its superiority proclaims Tombstone as a natural sanitarium, being in an altitude where the seasons are so happily blended that extremes in temperature and sudden changes of weather are practically unknown. An excellent view is afforded from the eminence of Tombstone hills; a grand panoramic view of miles of valley lands and mountain stretches lay before the astonished onlooker, and within easy distance some of the most historic points of interest are to be seen in the Dragoon mountain range, while the most magnificent scenic attractions in Arizona are to be found in the Huachucas, less than thirty miles distant. At Tombstone the climate attains the highest degree of perfection conducive to health and long life, while the summer months are altogether delightful.

GEORGE A. BEATON,
President American Finance and Securities Co.

CLOSELY connected with the management and immediately identified with the development and reopening of the properties of Tombstone Consolidated Mines Company, Limited, and one of the officers of the company to whom credit is due as an instrumental factor in their reopening, is Geo. A. Beaton, of New York City.

Mining owes much to the man whose perseverance and timely and well directed efforts have added material evidence to the fact that this field of enterprise is as much the realm of the business man and financier as it is of the speculator and investor. Mr. Beaton's manifest success in his other large interests pertaining to the art of industry and finance in which he has attained prominence and distinction, is a high tribute to his far-seeing judgment.

GEORGE A. BEATON.

PROMINENTLY IDENTIFIED WITH THE EXTENSIVE OPERATIONS OF THE TOMBSTONE MINES AND OTHER ARIZONA INTERESTS.

He is president of the American Finance and Securities Company, besides being a largely interested member and executive of the Development Company of America, a company that has done much in exploiting Arizona mines.

As a member of the executive committee of the board of directors of the Tombstone Consolidated Mines Co., Ltd., he is lending his great force and fostering influence in the direction of the company's interests, contributing largely to the ultimate success of the mammoth enterprise.

He is largely interested in vast eastern enterprises, and ever reading the book of human nature aright, has gathered about him men whose attributes comport well with his own exceptional ability, and it is a matter of pride that a man of his influence and worth should be so intimately associated with an enterprise whose successful outcome is of vital interest and deep concern to Tombstone.

Tombstone's Enterprising Business Men

TO THE modest, unassuming professional and business men every community owes its prosperity, its good name—in short, its very being. They are the rank and file of the great host of industry that is known as Progress. Because of the ties that bind them to their city, they can not become careless of its interests or standing in the eyes of the world. As the individual is jealous of the good repute of his home, and desirous for the betterment of its members, so is the business man zealous for the enhancement of the communal reputation, and ever alert for opportunity to advance his city's interests. The community of interests that the business man creates, and for which he stands, is the basic principle of civilization, and has contributed much towards its founding and upbuilding. They are all reliable, upright and public-spirited men, whose biographies—although necessarily abbreviated in these pages by lack of space—would be an adornment to a much more pretentious volume. Their reputations are firmly established throughout the Southwest, are a known quantity, and need no printed endorsement; but without their names this work would be incomplete, would be without its essential interest. THE PROSPECTOR is secure in its prediction that in the future Tombstone will retain the reputation it long has borne, of being Arizona's most liberal and public-spirited community.

F. N. WOLCOTT.

Highly Esteemed Tombstone Merchant and a Substantial Mercantile Institution.

ONE of the foremost institutions in every city is the general merchant's store, where all and sundry of the necessaries, conveniences and comforts of life are to be had under the same roof. Indeed, measured by the

proportion of the population that it reaches and whose wants are supplied from its varied stock, one might say without fear of successful contradiction that the store where general merchandise is sold leads them all. Certainly no other branch of business has so many or so constant patrons. Staples, or articles of necessity, control the markets of the world; other articles are merely auxiliary, while staples are the essentials. One of the most prominent houses engaged in this line of business

THE WOLCOTT BLOCK AND HOME OF THE LARGE WOLCOTT DEPARTMENT STORE.

in Tombstone is that owned by F. N. Wolcott. The Wolcott building is substantial and architecturally attractive, as the photographic reproduction herewith attests. His establishment has been a permanent feature of Tombstone's commercial life for many years. It was originally located on Fourth street, but he was obliged to move it to its present commodious premises to make room for his increased business. Mr. Wolcott is a pioneer of Tombstone, having settled here twenty-two years ago. He has always been one of its foremost citizens, and has been no small factor towards its advancement. He was elected probate judge of this county in 1890 and discharged the duties of that office in an exceptionally creditable manner. While he was an incumbent of that office the estates passing through his hands received the same trustworthy care that has distinguished his record as a business man. He is at all times deeply interested in the welfare of the public schools and has contributed much to their present efficiency. He has served this school district as school trustee for ten years, and is an old and honored member of the Ancient Order of Workmen. He has a wife and three children—Eva, Lucie and Newton. His eldest daughter, Miss Eva Wolcott, attends the Girls' Collegiate School of California.

PAUL B. WARNEKROS.

Pioneer Merchant and Representative Citizen—Honor of Tombstone's Oldest Resident.

THROUGHOUT the industrial life of this region there are few examples of success through sheer personal ability that can compare with the business career of Paul B. Warnekros. By energy, perseverance and integrity in all his dealings, he has built up a mercantile establishment that extends its trade throughout the county and is a credit to the city of its location. Mr. Warnekros is preeminently Tombstone's pioneer, being the first settler among those now living here. Although this city has seen dark and cheerless days since he first chose it as his home,

mant energies to the attention of those who could reopen her mines, and has ever sought to infuse trust in those who would have doubt. He came to Tombstone in March, 1878, and from the beginning was recognized as one of

P. B. WARNEKROS.

its most progressive spirits. He has been elected mayor, and justified the trust reposed in him by giving the city a clean and able administration. Although his commercial and mining interests have occupied his time to the exclusion of any active participation in politics, he has ever remained alert to the interests of his community, and has always been prominently identified with any movement tending to its advancement. His business is much wider

PAPAGO INDIAN CAMP—REGULAR SUMMER VISITORS TO DISPOSE OF OLLAS, POTTERY, ETC.

he has never entertained the least doubt that the once great mining camp was still potent of success, and that her future was assured. He has never flagged in his efforts to organize measures that would bring Tombstone's dor-

in its scope than the average mercantile establishment, comprising an extensive stock of farming implements and the innumerable miscellaneous articles required to supply the demands of the mining industry. Among other local property holdings he owns Schieffelin Hall, which, in addition to its historic associations, is one of the largest of Tombstone's buildings. Mr. Warnekros comes of sturdy Teuton stock and is fifty-three years of age. He is a substantial and public spirited citizen in all that the term implies, and deserves the esteem in which he is held by the people of Tombstone and Cochise county.

YAPLE & MORENO.

A Successful Tombstone Business Firm.

A BUSINESS peculiarly adapted to the needs of Tombstone is the firm of Yaple & Moreno. They display a splendid line of dry goods and furnishings, in addition to which they carry a first-class assortment of confectionery and a well-selected and complete stock of stationery. The

near Fifth. His first business was destroyed by fire, as was also the place he re-established on Allen street; but undaunted by disasters, and ever inspired by firm trust in the future of the community he had assisted in founding, he has continued to be a factor of importance in Tombstone's industrial life. Not only has Mr. Yaple been a trusted citizen and a business man of recognized ability and integrity, but throughout the long period of the once great mining camp's inactivity he has never abandoned his trust in the eventual reawakening into prosperity that is at last here. The family of Mr. Yaple comprises wife and daughter, the latter, Miss Nella Yaple, being the efficient manager of the Western Union Company's interests at Tombstone.

The junior member of the above firm is a splendid example of the steady, energetic young man, who, by eschewing the frivolous side of youth, builds in early manhood the

INTERIOR VIEW OF YAPLE & MORENO'S WELL-EQUIPPED ESTABLISHMENT.

firm was established in 1902, and is modern in every detail of management and stock. The proprietors are men who have had wide experience in everything appertaining to their branch of industry, are public-spirited citizens of this city, and have the confidence and trust of the entire community.

F. N. Yaple, the firm's senior member, is a respected pioneer of Tombstone. He was born sixty years ago in New York, and came to Tombstone in 1880 with an enviable record as a progressive and useful citizen of the Empire state. He was connected with the Great American Tea Company, gaining by his service with that great metropolitan establishment a wealth of experience that could not be obtained with less extensive concerns. He taught school, and later had supervision of the stationery department of the famous Eastman Business College, of Poughkeepsie. His first business venture in Tombstone was in the sewing machine line, and was located on Fremont street,

foundation of a broad and successful career. Although only twenty-five years of age, Frank Moreno is already recognized as an integrant member of this municipality, self-made and enterprising. He has had experience in plenty, having seen service with the best firms of the county—in Pearce, Tombstone, and in the Copper Queen store in Bisbee. He also was in charge of the Copper Queen's mercantile business in Nacosarri, Mexico. The accompanying cut is a good illustration of the firm's business house.

PERRY WILDMAN & CO.

A Creditable Mercantile Establishment That Is Winning Success.

THERE is no branch of commerce in which Tombstone gives more evidence of life and vigor, or in which she shows a healthier growth, than in the grocery trade.

The firm of Perry Wildman & Company is an instance in point. It does a large business in groceries and provisions in this city and surrounding country, and carries in its line one of the most complete and up-to-date stocks in

several mercantile enterprises throughout the territory, he served Maricopa county in the Eighteenth Legislature in an honest and efficient manner. He came to Tombstone in May, 1902, and his energy and knowledge of his business

THE FRONT OF PERRY WILDMAN & CO.'S ATTRACTIVE STORE.

Southern Arizona; and its reputation for progressiveness and fair dealing is such that its trade is rapidly on the increase. The cut on this page gives a good impression of the architectural beauty and modern construction of the firm's building.

Perry Wildman, who is fifty-four years of age, came to Arizona in 1880, first settling in Silver King, the then famous silver camp. Besides having been identified with

is attested by the large concern in which he is interested. His business associate, Mr. Edward Roberts, comes here from Kingman with an enviable record as a modern and square-dealing man of business affairs. Like all other well-informed men, Mr. Roberts has decided that Tombstone's future is assured, and has backed his judgment by investing his money in what is one of the city's foremost enterprises.

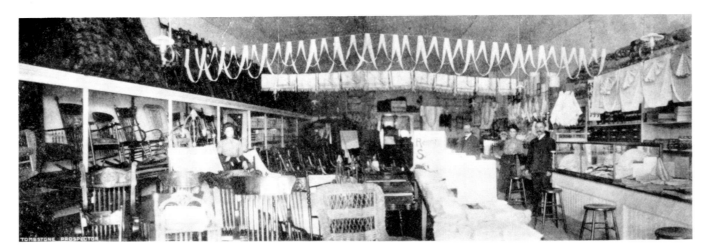

PEOPLE'S CASH STORE—A GLIMPSE OF THIS FURNISHINGS EMPORIUM.

AN ENTERPRISING FIRM.

The People's Cash Store a Leading Mercantile Business Identified With Tombstone.

THE People's Cash Store is a new mercantile corporation which came among us about six months ago, strongly endorsed. The stocks carried by this company rival in variedness and novelty the modern stores in larger cities. Dry goods and ladies' furnishings, in connection with everything up to the minute in men's wear, are their specialties, and added to this is a splendidly equipped furniture department. The constantly growing popularity of this ever-striving-to-improve concern is proof positive that

founded in 1879. Its proprietor, John Henninger, gives his personal supervision to the care of his patrons, contributing largely by his painstaking efforts to the success enjoyed by his branch of his business. The bill of fare embraces all that the market affords, together with the season's fish and game, which are served in an excellent manner by the best help to be obtained in Arizona. As a result of its efficiency, its business has been on the increase since its inception. Mr. Henninger is fifty years old. He came to Tombstone in 1886, and is a substantial citizen of this community. He is a Mason, and stands high in the councils of that society. This photograph tells eloquently of the Henninger building's fine structure and advantageous location.

INTERIOR VIEW OF TOMBSTONE'S PIONEER RESTAURANT—JOHN HENNINGER, PROP.

the People's Cash Store will be one of the leading mercantile establishments of the Southwest. Its success rests in the able management of Carl Behn, who is also secretary and treasurer of the enterprising concern, and who is a business man of large experience.

CAN CAN RESTAURANT.

A Famous Restaurant, With Excellent Cuisine.

IN ENUMERATING the business enterprises of cities due attention must, of course, be bestowed on those that provide for the convenience and comfort of the public. All cities pride themselves on the possession of popular places for satisfying the wants of the inner man. All the appointments of the Can Can, of Tombstone, are elegant and in artistic taste; and no more attractive restaurant will be found in any city in the Southwest. The building is large and commodious, and its cuisine is excellent. It is situated at the corner of Allen and Fourth streets, and was

THE CRYSTAL PALACE.

One of Tombstone's Historic Landmarks—Interior Fittings.

THE Crystal Palace Saloon, in point of historical association is probably one of the most interesting business places in Tombstone. In the days of this city's vivid past the Crystal Palace was always crowded with a motley throng that made up the camp's cosmopolitan population. Its faro lay-outs were the foci of bunches of dust-grimed freighters, bearded and red-shirted miners, sombreroed cowpunchers, business men, tourists, Mexicans, and the innumerable other types of the silver camp's first days. Thousands of dollars have changed hands within its walls, and more than once its echoes rang to the quick-shooting bad men who have gone forever. Although one of Tombstone's early buildings, it has the largest bar-rooms in the territory, and its elegant fixtures and costly furnishings make it a popular resort. Its present proprietors, Speck, Robbins and

Maden, are all up-to-date saloon men of long, varied experience. Mr. Speck was here in the camp's early days, and was also a pioneer and well-known business man of Prescott and Silver City. Mr. Robbins has been identified with the ownership and management of some of the Southwest's leading resorts; while Mr. Maden is well known throughout Arizona, and, moreover, was engaged in business in Nome and Dawson. He was in Alaska five years, and organized several successful mining companies there. He was one of the pioneers of Albuquerque, New Mexico, whose first hotel he built and owned. He was one of the foremost and influential citizens of that city, serving that county in the official capacity of commissioner. The accompanying cut of the Crystal Palace bar furnishes an idea of its attractiveness.

of quiet and domestic tastes. Nevertheless, he is a representative citizen, always ready to forward by his assistance any movement tending to Tombstone's advancement. The half-tone cut appearing herewith is from a photograph of the Marrs' residence at the corner of First and Safford streets.

W. R. KING.

Substantial Tombstone Citizen and Proprietor of King's Blacksmith Shop.

THE human race has ever evinced a deep interest in the rugged man whose industrial emblem is the ringing anvil. Since Tubal Cain swung his mighty sledge in the dim and distant days of the world's beginning. no

RESIDENCE OF JAMES MARRS.

JAMES H. MARRS.

One of Tombstone's Frontiersmen and Early Day Pioneers.

JAMES H. MARRS, or "Jim" as his host of friends prefer to know him, although a comparatively young man, is a Tombstone pioneer of the earliest settlers, having come here in 1879. In those distant days, although young in years, he was already a seasoned frontiersman, having had a past replete with Indian experiences. His first work in Tombstone was with the historical freighting system owned by "Jimmy" Carr, the foremost overland mule-train operator of the Southwest's industrial beginning. Mr. Marrs established his present place of business, the Pony saloon, six years ago, and by reason of his own affable presence, as much as by diligent attention to the wants of his patrons, has made it one of Tombstone's most popular resorts. Although he is a vigorous and active member of the Tombstone Fire Department, and is foreman of the Rescue Hose Company, he takes no active part in politics, being a man

unit of civilization, unless it be the soldier, has evoked so much attention from chronicler and poet as has the blacksmith. This interest, as is always the case where enduring concern is inspired by a class, is founded on public utility. The two pillars of civilization, the plow and the sword, were first made by the smithy. But, historic interest aside, the blacksmith's trade has taken enormous strides in the last decade. The modern, up-to-date blacksmith must have a shop that is in reality a factory, wherein he can build on demand anything, from a miner's candlestick to a ponderous freight wagon. Such a plant is the place of business of W. R. King, a cut of which appears on this page. Mr. King, as well as being an exceptionally thorough mechanic, is one of this city's pioneers. Away back in the eighties, when the big mule trains plied between Tombstone and the outside world, he had supervision of construction and repairs of the extensive rolling stock of J. E. Durkee & Co.'s freighting system, and that he was an efficient man at his calling is evident from the circumstance of his having been in charge of the fifteen mechanics then employed by that company. Mr. King is forty-two years of age. Although he has always been a representative citi-

cal honors. By close application and thorough understanding of business principles of his craft, he has built up a

INTERIOR VIEW OF W. R. KING'S MODERN BLACKSMITH ESTABLISHMENT.

THE GROCERY DEPARTMENT OF THE SOUTHWESTERN COMMERCIAL COMPANY.

zen, with a betterment of his environment ever at heart, he has been too engrossed with his own work to seek politi-

blacksmithing and wagon manufacturing plant that is unsurpassed by any like establishment in the country.

SOUTHWESTERN COMMERCIAL CO.

Tombstone Branch of an Extensive Commercial Firm.

THE present age is a busy and progressive one. With keen competition in all lines of business so energetic and viligant, it requires the utmost perseverance and en-

dise business. The firm whose name heads this article, by businesslike methods, is impelling favorable recognition. The Southwestern Commercial Company, with Mr. L. E. Fellows as manager, established here recently, has made an auspicious beginning. It is a large up-to-date concern, being a branch of a huge enterprise whose stores and warehouses include nearly a dozen cities in Arizona and the

BUSINESS PLACE OF TOMBSTONE'S "EXCLUSIVE MEN'S OUTFITTER"—JOHN ROCK, PROP.

terprise to gain success and keep pace with the times. But while this is proverbially true, there are instances where unceasing perseverance, long trained experience and thor-

republic of Mexico. The company's establishment, located in the Armory Block, already carries a large stock, and will increase it in the near future to include mining and

THE L. W. BLINN LUMBER CO.—EXTENSIVE YARDS AT TOMBSTONE.

ough knowledge arise superior to competition and insure success. In no branch of business do these factors of success apply with more force than in the general merchan-

milling supplies. Mr. Fellows has had a wide and varied experience in his line, and was the president and the manager of the large, well equipped institution in Johannesburg, California, known as the Fellows Mercantile Company. The accompanying illustration gives a conception of the Southwestern Commercial Company's attractive store and its complete and first-class stock.

JOHN ROCK.

Popular Business Firm Which Is Constantly Forging to the Front.

WITHIN the past decade a most important change has been effected in men's furnishings. From small and unassuming proportions as a mere department of dry goods stores, this branch of industry has come to be considered an important factor in the commercial trade of any city. The inconvenience attending delay and misfits, the advantages of procuring, at short notice, a complete outfit in this line, the ability to supply articles as good and as cheap as can be procured elsewhere—is the object of modern business methods, and led to the establishment

BLINN LUMBER CO.

Well Equipped Tombstone Branch of a Business Enterprise Whose Interests Extend Throughout the Southwest.

IN ALL cities noted for enterprise and progress in commercial affairs and growth in population, there are no more efficient and substantial contributors toward those desirable ends than those branches of industry that are connected with the building interests; for through their enterprise and exertions cities are built up, adorned and made attractive.

The L. W. Blinn Lumber Company is, without exception, the most extensive industry in the Southwest, extending over a score of towns and cities of California, Arizona and New Mexico. They supply Puget Sound pine and red wood lumber, railroad ties, telegraph poles, doors, sash and general building material, carrying as complete a stock in their line as may be found anywhere in the territory.

THE HANDSOME CRYSTAL PALACE LIQUOR COMPANY'S BAR.

of John Rock's business in Tombstone. Mr. Rock has been identified with public and other interests throughout the Southwest. He was for five years connected with the police department of the city of Phœnix, and was later employed by the Melzer Mining Company of Sonora, being their agent. He came to Tombstone in 1902, and that he has confidence in the city's future is shown by the extensive stock he has placed in his business. His well appointed and modern establishment embraces a good stock of men's furnishings and is assured a large future increase and success. His house is a pleasant and profitable one with which to establish business relations, commanding the respect of the trade, and the high regard of the community at large. Mr. Rock is thirty-three years old, and was married in January, 1901. Mrs. Rock, who is a popular young matron of Tombstone's society, was formerly Miss Josephine Stewart, of Phœnix.

J. N. Fisher, manager of the company's interests in this city, is an energetic and thoroughly competent lumberman, possessing a fund of experience in the lumber business that extends over the greater part of the United States, and has occupied many years of his life. He was fifteen years with the R. J. Hurley Lumber Company, of Kansas City, Mo., one of the largest lumber supply companies in the United States. He was also connected with the largest lumber companies in California for a period extending over three years, his experience in the trade aggregating altogether twenty years. Obviously, Mr. Fisher must know everything worth learning concerning the lumber business, and is thoroughly competent, enjoying both the confidence and esteem of his employers and all who know him in Tombstone. The company's Tombstone yard and office, on Toughnut street, has been faithfully reproduced in the half-tone appearing herewith.

TOMBSTONE IMPROVEMENT CO.

A Local Organization Prominent in Tombstone's Commercial Activity.

THE upbuilding and development of any city is largely contributed by the determination and never-failing efforts put forth by its citizens, and when this confidence is backed by heavy investments of collective local capital it bespeaks much for the community and its importance can not be overestimated. The Tombstone Improvement Company is a prominent factor in the industrial history of

plant and electricity are early auxiliaries also contemplated by the company, and their company building is both architecturally attractive and a substantial evidence of their confidence. Mr. Ben Goodrich is president of the corporation, is one of Arizona's foremost attorneys and enjoys to an eminent degree the respect of Tombstonites, among whom he is numbered as a worthy and influential pioneer, and has been honored as their ablest representative in various official capacities. The immediate management of the varied interests of this enterprise is conducted by C. D. Gage, who is secretary and general manager of the company. He is an active, energetic young man, fully alive to the best inter-

GAS PLANT OF THE TOMBSTONE IMPROVEMENT CO.

Tombstone, and entitled to more than ordinary consideration in the compilation of a work having for its object an historical review of the mercantile and industrial resources of the city. With the installation of the mammoth pumps of the Tombstone Consolidated Mines Company to drain the lower levels, and assurance had of abundance of supply, a local water system was instituted by the Improvement Company at considerable expense, a modern plant and equipment being secured, while its water mains form a network of pipes throughout the city. Water is supplied from the mines under contract, and its unquestioned purity and material reduction in cost of supply for domestic and irrigation purposes has won for the company a host of patrons. A recent test of the water, made for the company by Thomas Price & Son, analytical chemists, of San Francisco, shows the water to be organically pure. The company also owns the large gas plant that supplies Tombstone with light, and an excellent half-tone reproduction of a portion of the plant appears herewith. The company, in keeping abreast of the march of progress, are also installing one of the largest and withal modern ice plants in the Southwest, upon the completion of which its product will become a precious commodity at a price within the reach of all. A cold storage

ests of the company, and by earnest and persistent work has won the unbounded confidence and esteem reposed in him.

CUMMINGS & YORK.

A Successful Butchering Firm Supplying the Wants of the Public.

THE firm of Cummings & York, known as the City Meat Market, an interior view of whose business place is shown in the excellent half-tone reproduction on this page, is one of Tombstone's most enterprising business houses. Although possessing no competitors in their branch of industry, their dealings with the public are characterized by a policy of courteous treatment that has gained for them the respect of the entire community and causes a steady increase of business they enjoy.

C. L. Cummings is a native of Oxford, Chenango county, New York, where he was born in 1855. He came to Tombstone May 25, 1880, and with the exception of three and one-half years spent in charge of the water works at Charleston and a prosperous business venture in Bisbee, has been a respected and influential member of this community ever since. His present business extends back over fifteen years. Besides having large property interests in Tombstone, he is an owner of two successful cattle ranches, one in the Sulphur Spring valley, and the Box Canyon ranch in the Chiricahua mountains. He also possesses valuable mining properties in the Swisshelm mountains. Mr. Cummings is one of the staunch residents of Tombstone, being an example of what a man may accomplish by thrift, energy and diligent attention to business. In 1894 he was nominated for assemblyman and elected by a heavy majority, serving as chairman of the stock committee, and was largely instrumental in the defeat of the

F. H. CHRISTY.

Architect of Ability, Whose Work Is Well Known in the West.

IN PREPARING for the perusal of readers at home and abroad historical and descriptive notes on the representative industries and commercial enterprises of Tombstone it is important to select institutions and establishments whose success has contributed in large degree to the improvement of the city as a whole. There are few per-

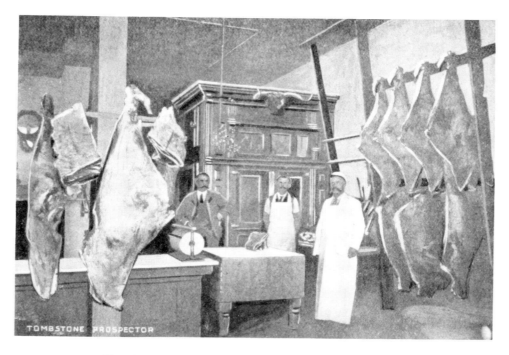

VIEW OF THE CUMMINGS & YORK UP-TO-DATE MEAT MARKET.

movement for county division. He also served two years as city treasurer, discharging the duties of that office with integrity and ability. He is a member of the Independent Order of Odd Fellows, is a married man, having been wedded in 1900 to Miss Ida Padfield, of Los Angeles, and has one son.

Thomas R. York is an Arizonan of the pushing, energetic type; finding time in the midst of many business interests to take a hand in public affairs and contribute the training of a successful business man to the county's interests. In addition to his local property and business, he has long been known throughout the county as a successful cattle man, and has, besides his Huachuca cattle ranch, some promising mining properties. He was elected to the board of supervisors of Cochise county, of which he is chairman, in 1900. Being the hold over or long term candidate, he has still almost two years of service in that office to fulfill. His tenure in public office has been marked by wise and just discrimination in all matters concerning the welfare of the county. He entered the firm of Cummings & York in 1901, and although he holds property interests elsewhere, is a pioneer of this city, having come here in 1879. Mr. York was married to Miss Minnie Brown, of Huachuca, ten years ago. They have five children, Maude, Dorothy, Beulah, Nora and Roland.

sons in Tombstone who have in so short a time risen into such prominence or deserve more favorable mention than F. H. Christy. He is one of the most competent architects and thorough mechanics in the Southwest. In Los Angeles, where he lived for twenty years, he was a member of the Los Angeles Builders' Exchange and a prominent contractor. Coming to Arizona, he first established a business in Globe, where he remained for six years. During his stay there his ability in the building line made his services widely sought for. The Miners' Union Hall and the Butler Block, fine substantial edifices of the Gila county copper camp, were erected by him. Since coming to Tombstone he has done much satisfactory work in his line, the two best examples being the fine building now occupied by the firm of Wildman & Company, and his own residence on Safford street, a beautiful illustration of modern architecture. Mr. Christy is a Knight of Pythias, and is thirty-eight years old. He is a married man, having wedded Miss Marian A. McLaughlin, of Kansas City, seven years ago. The cut published herewith of the Christy residence is eloquent of the skill in architectural work possessed by its owner and builder. Mr. Christy has some other large building contracts on hand and by giving his personal supervision to his contract work, gives universal satisfaction and is winning an enviable reputation.

HOTEL NOBLES.

A New Hotel, With Excellent Accommodations.

A N IMPORTANT item of information for the visitor to Tombstone, whether he come from adjoining parts of the county or from still farther afield, is where he may located, newly furnished, and is modern and up-to-date in every detail of its appointment. Gene Nobles, its proprietor, came here recently from Prescott. Mr. Nobles has been injured twice in the past—once while in the railroad service, and, later, when acting as superintendent of the Telluride Electric Light and Power Company, of Telluride, Colorado, he accidently received a current of electricity

RESIDENCE OF F. H. CHRISTY.

find comfortable accommodation during his sojourn in the city—where, in short, he will be made to feel most at home. Tombstone has no lack of comfortable hostelries where one may find excellent quarters, and the Hotel Nobles is espe- that has left him an invalid, who can move about only by aid of a propelling chair. However, in spite of his infirmity, Mr. Nobles remains watchful that nothing is omitted that might add to the comfort of his guests. His charges

THE COMMODIOUS QUARTERS OF THE HOTEL NOBLES.

cially equipped for the requirements of the traveling public. It is situated in the Gird and Mining Exchange blocks, of which it occupies the entire second stories. It is centrally are reasonable, and those who visit Tombstone would do well to bear the Hotel Nobles in mind, the traveling public finding everything especially for their convenience.

S. DUNCKEL.

Expert Paper Hanging and Prominent Contractor of High Class Interior Decorations.

S. DUNCKEL, a good photo of whom is herewith shown, is a paperhanger and decorator whose artistic and reliable work has gained for him a wide patronage. He

extensive establishments in various parts of the country, employing as many as ten men in one business. He had charge of the painting, marbleizing and tinting in the interior finishing of the Copper Queen hotel of Bisbee, the copper camp's largest and most artistically finished building. He also has papered and decorated many prominent residences in Bisbee, Douglas and neighboring towns. He established his business here in 1902, and the high class

INTERIOR VIEW OF W. A. KING'S SALOON.

first pursued his calling in Butte, Montana, where he possessed a large establishment. He is a young man, being

S. DUNCKEL.

thirty-three years old, and is thoroughly modern in every detail pertaining to his vocation. He has owned some

work done by him is steadily increasing his patronage. Mr. Dunckel's Allen street business places carries an excellent stock of wall paper and the other materials used in tinting, varnishing and all kinds of interior and exterior furnishings.

W. A. KING.

A Typical Westerner With Early Day Experiences.

IN THE early stages of its development the West demands men of tireless physique and indifference to danger—men who will forego the comforts of civilization for the zest to be obtained from precarious life in the saddle. Without that rugged class the Apache and the outlaw would prove an insuperable bar to the Southwest's development. Such a man is W. A. King, or "Billy," as he is popularly known by his acquaintances. He was born in Rapide parish, Louisiana, thirty-nine years ago, but came to the West when a boy. He was a hard-riding ranger of Captain McMurray's celebrated troop when the life of a ranger was all that the name implies. He came to this county in 1883, first settling at San Simon. He served for some time as foreman of the Huachuca Cattle Company, known as the Snake ranch. He also served as peace officer in this county under Sheriffs Kelton, White and Slaughter, and has been identified as a business man in various parts of the county. He conducted the Grand Central Hotel, of Benson, in a creditable manner, and later was instrumental in establishing the custom house at La Morita, about nine miles from Bisbee. He remained there several years, but eventually returned to the city of his first choice and entered his present business. A view of the interior of Mr. King's saloon appears herewith.

BEN HENEY.

THE past history of Fairbank is not dissimilar to the exciting events that have made Tombstone famous, and with the railroad connecting the short distance, her interests are linked in unison, and harmonious business relations exist between the county seat and her neighboring suburb. Fairbank is an important commercial point, and a mercantile establishment that has been identified with the community for many years, commanding an enviable distinction in business circles, is the Fairbank Commercial Company. Mr. Ben Heney, of whom a half-tone is herewith represented, is heavily interested in the company and is the manager of this extensive enterprise, whose success is well merited because of attentive interest, ability, energy and strict business management. Mr. Heney is an old Arizonan and is well and favorably known. He was a resident of Pima county for many years and attained prominence in political affairs, having served in official capacity on numerous occasions in that county.

BEN HENEY.

He has twice been elected to the important position of county treasurer and tax collector and has served eight years as secretary of the territorial board of equalization. Mr. Heney is an adherent of Republican principles and has made his influence felt in party work. Besides his wholesale and retail interests at Fairbanks. Mr. Heney owns some valuable mining properties and is an enterprising factor in the upbuilding of the country in which he has become identified.

GEORGE H. McKENZIE.

An Arizona Pioneer With Interesting Early Day Reminiscences.

GEORGE H. McKENZIE, proprietor of the Drop In saloon, of this city, has a past of frontier hardships and experiences that would supply material for a romance

GEORGE H. M'KENZIE.

of the West. He is an Arizona pioneer of the very first vintage, having come to Yuma as long ago as 1868. In those days the city of Castle, up the Gila a few miles from Yuma, was a booming little city, deriving its existence from rich placer diggings. Placering was also lining the banks of the Colorado river with a busy throng of goldseekers from Yuma to Castle Dome, a distance of twenty-eight miles. It was also in the year of Mr. McKenzie's arrival at Yuma that the territorial prison was built there. The first freight—machinery—ever destined for Arizona was brought up the Colorado river to Yuma by his father, Captain C. H. McKenzie, a fine example of the early days' steamboat captain, who, at the hale old age of seventy-three, is still in active service along the coast of New Zealand. He has been captain of his own vessel for fifty years. Mr. McKenzie has also seen steamboat service, having been associated with his father in the business in early youth. He is a Hassayamper of the old school. He was in business in Ehrenberg over thirty years ago, was deputy city marshal of Phœnix from 1880 to 1882, and is one of the best known and most experienced saloon men in the territory, having always borne the reputation of conducting an orderly and reputable house. Besides his local business, he has mining interests in Cochise and Santa Cruz counties. Mr. McKenzie is fifty-five years old, and is a member of the Red Men, belonging to Cochise Tribe, No. 7, of Bisbee. The accompanying photograph is a good picture of the subject of this sketch.

JOHN MONTGOMERY.

JOHN MONTGOMERY—"Honest John," as he is known throughout the Southwest—although a busy business man, by the energy, system and persevering integrity displayed by him as a public officer has made a reputation for himself that will endure in Arizona's history. By sheer force of merit he has won a place of lasting trust in the hearts of Cochise county's people. He comes from the state of Ohio, where he was born July 15, 1831. He followed placer mining in California and the Northwest from 1852 to 1874, was a resident of New Mexico four years, and came to Tombstone in January, 1879. He has resided here continuously since then, being engaged in the livery and feed

acterized by the same resolute adherence to honesty that has distinguished his many years in the public's service.

TOMBSTONE DRUG CO.

A Modern and Well Equipped Tombstone Pharmacy.

NO MAN occupies a more responsible position or is intrusted with more vital interests than the druggist. In the obtruce art of preparing medicines the layman is compelled perforce to trust blindly to the knowledge of drugs held by the specialized training of the pharmaceutist. In filling a prescription an inexperienced druggist by the smallest inaccuracy in compounding the substances

PANORAMIC VIEW

stable business. He was elected to the board of supervisors in 1882, and served in that capacity with ability and distinction for four years. In 1888 he was again chosen to represent the county's voters in that office, and again served four years. In 1892 he was nominated by his party for the office of county treasurer, but was defeated by the strong Democratic majority of that year. He was appointed to fill a vacancy in the board of supervisors, March 19, 1895, serving almost a full term, or one year nine and one-third months. He was elected a member of the board a third time by the heaviest vote on either ticket, again serving four years, aggregating nearly fourteen years of service for Cochise county in one official capacity. Mr. Montgomery and his colleagues in office so handled the affairs of this county that its bonded indebtedness was reduced $100,000, thereby making a reduction in annual interest from $17,990, as paid in 1889, to $8,260, payable after January 15, 1901. Mr. Montgomery's public record needs no comment; it speaks for itself, and his business interests have been char-

used in its composition might imperil the life of a human being; and this only one of many reasons that necessitate a thorough knowledge of the elements of his art by the successful pharmacist. Mr. Ed. Flach, proprietor of the Tombstone Drug Company, is a perfect and up-to-date pharmaceutical chemist, being a graduate of the Ontario College of Pharmacy, of Ontario, Canada. He has furthermore been qualified for successful practice of his calling by eight years of metropolitan experience, gained in connection with some of the most prominent pharmacies in Chicago. His drug store is most completely equipped, and is a source of pride to the city in which it has been established. He carries, in connection with his drug supplies, an extensive line of cigars, ivory goods, toilet articles, candies and the innumerable other articles sold by modern pharmacies. The circumstance of a young man of Mr. Flach's education and experience choosing this community as a field in which to build up a business is a good illustration of the universal confidence in Tombstone.

MAYOR A. WENTWORTH.

A Popular Official With a Long and Useful Public Career.

FEW men have been more closely identified with the public life of Tombstone than A. Wentworth. He has served the city and county in various capacities, and has always borne a reputation as an exemplar of official life. He came to Cochise county in 1885, and for seven years held the important position as agent of the New Mexico & Arizona Railroad, at Fairbank, where he was also agent for Wells, Fargo & Company. He was first elected recorder of this county in 1892, and filled the office with honesty and ability, serving in that capacity two terms. He also oc-

F. B. AUSTIN.

F. B. AUSTIN is one of Tombstone's earlier pioneers, redolent of the days when the "hills were new," ere the safety and comforts of later civilization had arrived down here to stay. He had much experience as a placer miner, and invented a gold washer that has many points of interest. He is one of those sturdy pioneers who helped found what became the greatest mining metropolis the Southwest has ever known, and is brimming with reminiscences of the rough and ready days of yore, when only men made in heroic, staunch mold were needed on the turbulent border. He founded the Papago store of those days and made, as the saying goes, plenty of money; made

CITY OF TOMBSTONE.

cupied the position of county treasurer during two terms, establishing a record for efficiency and integrity during his incumbency. He is at present chief magistrate of this city, and is the first mayor of the Newer Tombstone, for he has been the first incumbent of that office to hear the locomotives' shrill clarion telling Tombstone's hills of the new day's advent. Although engaged in business, he still finds time to act as secretry of the Rescue Hose Company, being an enthusiastic member of the Tombstone Fire Department. He is the popular proprietor of the Tombstone Billiard Parlors, a half-tone illustration of whom, with the mayor and city officers, appear on these pages. Mr. Wentworth was born in Corlina, Maine, October 2, 1850. He is a Mason of an exalted degree; is a Knight of Pythias; a veteran member of the Ancient Order of the United Workmen, and foremost in matters pertaining to the city's advancement, being a public-spirited citizen who is held in high esteem both in the city of which he is the executive head and throughout the entire southwest.

it, too, by upright and fair methods, for in this community the name of F. B. Austin stands for honorable dealing. He has always been one of the most public spirited members of Tombstone, ever working faithfully for its advancement, and alert to anything that might contribute to its good repute and success. At one time Mr. Austin established a business in Tempe, where he also served in an official capacity, but later he returned to the city whose industrial bastions he had aided in building, and established a mercantile business, the Pioneer Store, in its present commodious situation, at the corner of Fremont and Fifth streets. Mr. Austin is a man of family, having a wife and two sons, Hosmer and Frank, thirteen and fifteen years of age respectively.

Having been so intimately identified with Tombstone's past, he is competent to judge of its future possibilities, and still trusts as firmly as he did all through its years of misfortune that it will again assume its place as one of the foremost of Arizona's cities.

A. L. GROW.

ANY history of Tombstone without the name of A. L. Grow would be woefully incomplete. As superintendent of the Tranquillity Mining Company, he kept that company employing a force of men when everything else in this district was closed, thus veritably keeping this community from total industrial death. His resolute and continued efforts have contributed hardly less than those of subsequent associates to the consolidation of the mining interests that eventually was consummated, and without which Tombstone's rehabilitation would have been impossible. Tombstone, therefore, owes A. L. Grow a debt of gratitude that can not be overestimated. Mr. Grow, of whom this half-tone reproduction is a good portrait, is one of Arizona's earliest pioneers, being a resident within the territorial boundaries for more than thirty-three years. He was one of the engineers of the Monadnock when that vessel rounded the Horn many years ago. He first came to Yuma; but in the days of Tombstone's beginning, when this was the port of entry, he was here serving as customs collector. He is sixty-six years of age, but is still a keen and active man, retaining all the vigor of his youth. He has been an active member of this community from its beginning, and richly merits the esteem in which he is held by all who know him. He is now one of the Tombstone school trustees, having always manifested a deep concern in the affairs of the local public school.

A. L. GROW.

M. C. BENTON.

M. C. BENTON is a representative citizen of Tombstone and Cochise county. A goodly portion of his forty-three years has been spent in the West, and his conduct as a citizen and public officer has gained for him the esteem of all who know him. Mr. Benton came to Arizona from Santa Fe, New Mexico, where he served six

years in the sheriff's office with ability and distinction. In 1894 he settled in Congress, but soon afterwards came to Cochise county, which he considers his home; and no one has more trust in this city's future prosperity. He is a first-class miner with a thorough knowledge of that vocation. In Bisbee, while employed as a timberman by the Copper Queen, he received an enduring reminder of that

M. C. BENTON.

hazardous calling by the loss of a finger. He was chairman of the board of supervisors of Cochise county during the term of 1898-1900, being the only Democrat elected to the board that year. During his incumbency of that office he fulfilled the judgment of this county's voters by diligent and competent attention to the interests of his constituency. His present business, the Headquarters Saloon, he established in 1900; and because of his uniformly courteous treatment of his patrons and its well-managed and orderly premises, it has been a success from its beginning. He also possesses valuable mining interests in this district—the Benton group, now being developed under bond, is one of several mining properties owned by him. Mr. Benton, whose excellent likeness illustrates this sketch, is a married man. His wife, whom he married in December, 1886, was Miss Edith King, of Santa Fe, New Mexico. They have two bright children, Samuel and Roy, aged fourteen and eleven years, respectively.

HENRY WALLACE, M. D.

DR. HENRY WALLACE, the subject of this sketch, is a graduate of the Brooklyn Polytechnic Institute, New York. He received the degree of Doctor of Medicine from the Long Island College Hospital, in 1890, and for the following year served as resident physician and surgeon in the same institution. He was shortly afterward appointed surgeon to the Out-Patient department, and assistant surgeon to St. John's Hospital, which position he held for ten years, when he was appointed laryngologist. He was for several years connected with the teaching department of the Long Island College Hospital—first in the department of obstetrics, and later in diseases of the throat and nose. Dr. Wallace served for several years as captain and assistant surgeon in the National Guard of New York state, and during the Spanish-American war was commissioned major and surgeon of the United States volunteers. The doctor

HENRY WALLACE, M. D.

was well known as a practitioner of medicine and surgery in New York, where he practiced since his graduation. He is a member in good standing of the principal medical and surgical societies in Brooklyn, New York, and has contributed quite extensively to medical literature. Dr. Wallace is a member of the Brooklyn Riding and Driving Club, and is an enthusiastic horseman. Since coming West he has been engaged in the practice of his profession in this city, besides being a director of the Bunker Hill Mining Company, of Tombstone, and secretary of the corporation. He has, both by his demonstrated ability as a successful practitioner and pleasing address, won for himself a host of friends in Tombstone.

The doctor has always taken a great interest in military matters, and is a member of the Association of Military Surgeons of the United States, and since his army service, of the Military and Naval Order of the Spanish-American War. The doctor will shortly return to his practice in the East, his visit to this country being rendered necessary by the health of one of the members of his family.

GEO. W. SEAVERNS.

GEORGE W. SEAVERNS is a fine type of the conservative Western mine operator. He came here from Boston, where he has large interests, in 1886, and during the seventeen years covering his operations in this county has contributed incalculably towards the advancement of his chosen field. Not only has he always been outspoken amongst Eastern investors, of his belief in this county's

natural resources, but he has also been instrumental in bringing much capital into this neighborhood. Every old-time resident of this county knows of the Seaverns property, at Gleason, in the Turquoise Mining District, but only a mining man can appreciate the able and conservative management that made the property successful under adverse circumstances. The mine was so wholly isolated from every base of supply, and so far from reduction works that the exorbitant freight rates were practically prohibitive. To overcome the heavy expense of shipping to distant points, Mr. Seaverns undertook the task of erecting a modern ten-stamp mill for treatment of its ores. His belief, founded on close examination of the structure of the country, that water with internal pressure existed below the surface, was proven correct by the first boring. Water was encountered at a depth of forty-eight feet, with pressure enough to force it to within eleven feet of the surface. The success of that well has demonstrated a condition that undoubtedly will be a large factor in future investments in that district.

At the age of sixty, Mr. Seaverns is still vigorous and alert to the interests of his many mining properties, and may be relied on to do much in the future for the interests of Cochise county. Although a Bostonian by birth and breeding, he is a typical Arizonan, with ever a good word to say for the territory. As coming from a close student of mining affairs, it is interesting to know that in

JAMES HAGAN.

common with all well-informed mining men, Mr. Seaverns feels certain of a successful future for Tombstone's mines.

JAMES HAGAN.

IN EVERY business, individuals are to be found whose personal standing is beyond cavil; whose record as citizens is exceptionally good; whose merited popularity with their fellow citizens makes their success in any business undertaking assured. Such is the position of James Hagan, who recently opened the popular resort known as the Arcadia. He is not only a representative citizen of this city, but is one of its sturdiest pioneers. He came here in 1881, from Nevada and California, where he had seen much experience as a mechanical engineer, and was one of the first engineers to handle a lever for the Toughnut Mill and Mining Company. He has been here during most of the years that have elapsed since then, and possesses a fund of historical incidents of the camp's palmy days. His bar is one of the neatest in external appearance and interior fittings in the city. His wife, Mrs. Jennie Hagan, resides in San Francisco, with her daughter, Miss Philomene Hagan.

H. T. FISHER.

H. T. FISHER, president and general manager of the Pittsburg-Arizona Gold and Copper Company, is one of Arizona's energetic mining men, as well as a pioneer of Tombstone. He came here in 1879, before the present city of Tombstone existed. He was in those days general manager of the Ground Hog Company's mine, one of the first two claims located by Ed. Schieffelin. Subsequently, he became general manager of the Sterling Silver Mining Company, first known as the Vizina, which, even before 1882, had produced more than half a million dollars' worth of bullion. Going East, he became a director of the Creighton Mining Company, of Cherokee, Georgia, and was general manager of the company's extensive operations. Later, he disposed of his Eastern interests and returned to

H. T. FISHER.

Arizona, where he resumed active mining. Mr. Fisher, whose picture appears with this sketch, is fifty-two years old, and, as he has many property interests in this section, will no doubt continue as useful a factor to the county's mining operations as he has been in the past. Mr. Fisher's worth as a mining expert may be judged from the fact that in the early history of the now famous Congress gold mine he recommended that property in opposition to the verdict of a prominent expert, who had pronounced it worthless. Mr. Fisher is actively interested in the Pitts-

burg-Arizona Company, of which he is the ruling spirit, and he is backing his confidence in the merits of his property by giving the same his personal attention.

TOMBSTONE TELEPHONE CO.

THE Tombstone Telephone Company is a significant example of the trust in Tombstone's future entertained by sagacious business men. They have installed a

A. G. SHARKEY.

plant that can not be surpassed in thoroughness of equipment and material, necessarily entailing an investment involving much money. The efficient gentleman in charge of this plant, A. G. Sharkey, whose picture appears with this article, is a typical example of the ability of the modern young man. Although only twenty-three years of age, he has become, by close application to the principles of his calling, as thorough an electrician as can be found anywhere. His first service in Arizona was with the Electrical Supply Company, of Phoenix. Since he acquired the knowledge of electrical application necessary to successful practice of his craft, Mr. Sharkey has held many important positions. Among others, he was connected with the Arizona Electric Company for three years, and was foreman of the Jerome Telephone and Telegraph Company for five months. He is at present local manager of the Tombstone Telephone Company, having assumed charge of its business immediately after its establishment. Although a native of California, Mr. Sharkey is in a nature a pioneer of this city, having resided here in the eighties, and is a nephew of Colonel Michael Grey, the notable pioneer legislator of Cochise county.

COCHISE COUNTY ABSTRACT CO.

CLYDE R. SEITZ, secretary of the Cochise County Abstract and Title Trust Company, is a good illustration of the self-reliant and competent young man in the world of industry. Although a young man, he has had much experience in the varied branches that are necessary to a mining engineer's craft. He was formerly with the Abstract and Title Company, of Deadwood, S. D., of which company his father, C. K. Seitz, a prominent and influential citizen of the Northern state, is secretary. He was also formerly assistant city engineer of the city of Deadwood, when its present splendid water system was installed. Subsequently, he took up abstract work, and has become one of the most thorough adepts of that trade, possessing, in fact, the only complete set of abstract books in Cochise county, and this fact makes it at once obvious that the company is well equipped to give prompt attention to abstract work. During the short time he has been

C. R. SEITZ.

established in Tombstone his pleasing personality, as well as his persevering attention to business, has gained for him a host of friends. Mr. Seitz is twenty-five years old. The accompanying cut is an excellent likeness.

C. W. BLACKBURN.

C. W. BLACKBURN is a well-known mining man of this county, and has a history replete with thrilling incidents of Arizona's turbulent past. He is a veteran of the Civil War, and when he first entered Arizona he crossed the desert alone on horseback from San Diego to Phœnix. When he arrived in what is now the territorial capital, in 1876, what is now the populous city of Phœnix was a little outpost of civilization, whose houses could be counted on the fingers of one hand. He served in the quartermaster's department at Yuma four years, from early in 1877 until late in 1880. He was in Tucson when the railroad first reached there, and came to Tombstone in the same year. He has ever since been closely identified with Cochise county's industrial life. He has been a successful business man both in Bisbee and Tombstone, and in later years has been a factor in some prominent Cochise county mining enterprises. His mining interests include several properties in this county and Sonora. The accompanying half tone shows the Blackburn residence and the beautiful rose bush that embowers it.

J. A. ROCKFELLOW.

J. A. ROCKFELLOW, civil engineer, than whom no one has been more closely identified in Tombstone's affairs, is also engaged in cattle raising in the Sulphur Spring valley. Although he has held important public positions in Arizona, having a splendid record as a public educator, he has been actively engaged in the cattle business for twenty years, or since 1883. Mr. Rockfellow is a native of New York state, whence he came to Arizona in 1878, and has been known here as a mining man and surveyor of ability. He is the present official surveyor of Cochise county, to which office he has been elected at various times. In 1889 and 1890 he was principal of Tombstone public schools, and filled that position with distinction. From 1895 until 1898 he occupied the position of professor of mathematics of the University of Arizona. Mr. Rockfellow is a man of upright character, of cultured and refined tastes, and is held in high regard by the people throughout the territory. A photo of the residence of Mr. Rockfellow appears among the group of Tombstone's residences.

E. P. A. LARRIEU.

E. P. A. LARRIEU, the genial and popular manager of the Montezuma Hotel, at Fairbank, of whom the above half tone is an excellent likeness, is twenty-six years of age. He has been a resident of this section for many years, is well and favorably known, enjoying a wide circle of acquaintanceship. Mr. Larrieu is an experienced hotel man, considerate and ever solicitous of the comfort of his guests, winning for him a place in the esteem and regard of all who know him. Mr. Larrieu also possesses literary attainments of merit, and is a young man of great possibilities in the journalistic field. He has acted in the capacity of correspondent for a number of journals, and demonstrated a natural aptness that doubtless later will

E. P. A. LARRIEU.

lead him into editorial work and direct his energies and influence in this channel of public usefulness.

SCOTT WHITE.

AMONG the prominent men of Arizona who have contributed in a large degree to the welfare of the territory, and who have been instrumental in its forward development, and who have striven zealously and with unflinching devotion to duty to the betterment and maintaining of the public good and respect of the community at large, is Scott White, treasurer of the La Cananea Consolidated Copper Mining Company, a man whose reputation for fearlessness and administrative ability in his official and private capacity has won him distinction as a popular and efficient officer. Mr. White was born in La Grange, Fayette county, Texas, the home of the brave and fearless men and the birthplace of daring spirits whose sons have long been known as men of courage. On coming to Arizona, in the year 1881, he engaged in the cattle business in Cochise county for many years with great success. By his warm hearted, genial disposition and generosity, a characteristic of the essentially Western man, and sincere belief in the future of his adopted home, he soon became a prominent and popular factor in the community where he lived. In 1886 he was elected a member of the territorial legislature and his services there were such as to warrant his supporters extreme satisfaction in their choice. For many years following his election to the legislature he filled many offices of public trust and responsibility and retained the utmost confidence reposed in him by the public. In 1890 he attained to the position of supervisor of Cochise county. In 1882 he was chosen to fill the office of sheriff of his county, which he held until appointed to the office of district clerk in 1894. Again in 1896 he was elected sheriff and it was during the administration of

SCOTT WHITE.

these offices that he became the fearless foe of the outlaw, whose daring deeds in this capacity won him great popularity. His affable, bonhommie manner and genial, sympathetic nature holds for him the sincere affection of all who know him, nor does he permit his success to estrange the friendships of former years. He retired from public life during his service as sheriff, to give his time to the several mining interests in Mexico and Arizona. As evidence of the trust reposed in him by the people of wealth and influence, may be mentioned his rise to the trustworthy position of treasurer of the La Cananea Consoli-

dated Copper Company of Mexico. Mr. White still calls Tombstone his home—a pardonable pride. He is married and has three children. A good likeness of Mr. White appears with this sketch and a view of the White residence also appears in the group of residences.

JOHN E. BACON, M. D.

DR. JOHN E. BACON occupies a place of high regard in Tombstone alike for his courteous personality and splendid professional attainments. Natural ability as-

JOHN E. BACON, M. D.

sociated with a brilliant education and extensive experience has contributed to making him one of Arizona's foremost physicians. He was born in Blossburg, Pennsylvania, thirty-five years ago, and graduated with the class of '88 from La Fayette college at Easton. Later he graduated from the medical department of the University of Pennsylvania and took up the practice of medicine with his father, an eminent physician of Wellsborough, Pennsylvania, whose wide practice and professional ability contributed incalculably to the efficiency that his son has since attained. The elder gentleman, at the hale age of sixty-seven, is still an active and valued practitioner. The subject of this sketch, after leaving Wellsborough, settled in Buffalo, New York, where he established a large and lucrative practice, but in 1898 he entered the service of the United States army in the capacity of surgeon and was stationed at Chickamauga Park, Georgia. In December, 1898, he was ordered to Fort Grant, Arizona, remaining there until 1901, when he resigned his position with the army to come to Tombstone. Since here he has secured, in addition to his position as physician of the Cochise county hospital, a practice that not only includes dwellers in the city limits, but many throughout the surrounding towns and country. In this connection it might be added that under his competent management the hospital of Cochise county has attained a degree of excellence unequaled by any like institution in Arizona. His office and laboratory are fitted up with all the medical and surgical appurtenances nowadays considered essential to the largest city practitioner's work, containing static electric and

X-Ray apparatus and all other appliances used in performing scientific operations. His adeptness in thermic treatment of chronic diseases, of which he is regarded as a specialist second to none, has contributed in a large degree to his present popularity. His hospital's thorough equipment and his natural skill in diagnosis and treatment make Dr. Bacon a physician without a superior in the territory. He was married in 1897 to Miss Grace James, of Elmira, New York, and make their home at their cozy and attractive residence on Fourth street. Dr. Bacon is also identified with the mining industry of Cochise county, being interested in a group of valuable gold claims in the Chiricahua mountains which has great promise and with development will be numbered among the early producers of that section.

years ago as an ink-smeared "devil" on the newspaper he afterwards came to control. The PROSPECTOR'S weekly edition is the far-famed TOMBSTONE EPITAPH, the journal whose editor Hoyt made a character in one of his inimitable plays.

In the PROSPECTOR'S store room are many newspaper souvenirs of this city's tumultuous past; but the most historic of them all is an old Washington hand press, Arizona's most notable relic. It is the very first printing press that came to Arizona, and its history is well worth perpetuation. If this old-timer could speak it no doubt would grumblingly complain against the life of ease it has been leading of late years; for the old utensil has had a turbulent and useful career. It was brought to Arizona in 1858, coming from the East by way of the Horn, and being

HOME OF THE TOMBSTONE DAILY PROSPECTOR.

THE "PROSPECTOR."

The Journal That Has Been Faithful to Tombstone, and Has Been an Essential Integer in Her History-Building Past.

Arizona's First Newspaper Press and Its Identification With Her Most Eventful Epochs.

THE TOMBSTONE PROSPECTOR was established in 1886. Founded in the palmiest days of the camp's golden past, it has remained faithful to Tombstone in her hours of stress and doubt, ever voicing her peoples' deep convictions of her mineral resources, ever eager to call quick attention to the occasional sunny rifts in the cloud that so long hung over its own city; and now that the sun of a prosperous day is rising for Tombstone, the PROSPECTOR rejoices with the rest, and is proud because at last the camp's worth is being verified. Its trust and devotion to Tombstone is only natural. William Hattich, its owner, has been a resident of the camp since childhood, working

freighted by wagon to Tubac, where its owner, Sylvester Mowry, Arizona's pioneer journalist, founded the *Arizonian*. Only a few issues had been published when the Civil War began. The United States troops were withdrawn from the territory, and, because of the Apaches' lack of interest in matters journalistic, the *Arizonian* was discontinued. William S. Oury, of Tucson, was the next owner of the type-jammer throughout the Civil War, and in 1867 he resumed publication of the *Arizonian*, with an itinerant type-sticker by name of Price as editor. Price succumbed to the tremendous mental strain of conducting that huge metropolitan daily, loaded up on aqua fortis and suspended publication. After Arizona's public opinion had plugged along a while without any moulding, Sidney R. DeLong, now one of the oldest and most respected of the territory's pioneers, assumed charge of the *Arizonian*, and piloted it through the remainder of '67 and '68, supporting McCormick for delegate to Congress during his first political campaign. After that memorable political joust the press was turned over to Mr. Doone, who displayed his knowledge of good English by dropping the second "i" from the name, leaving it "*Arizonan.*" Nevertheless, his action promoted one of the most heated and protracted arguments on the subject this pen-scarred old territory has ever known. Under Doone's rule the journal became Democratic, and in 1870 advocated the cause of Peter R. Brady. Later, Mr. DeLong

in so far as is within a newspaper's province—its good repute throughout the Southwest.

The accompanying illustration is a good reproduction of the PROSPECTOR's two-storied building on Fremont street, opposite the City Hall.

MUNICIPAL OFFICERS OF THE CITY OF TOMBSTONE.

again secured charge of the old press, and with it began publication of the Tucson *Citizen,* the oldest surviving offspring of the famous piece of machinery, with John Watson as editor. Later it found its way to Tombstone, and eventually became a part of the PROSPECTOR's plant, and will likely be preserved to the Pioneer Historical Society as a souvenir of the camp's past.

The PROSPECTOR's intimate acquaintance with Tombstone's past history, allied with natural affection and pride for its home, make it exceptionally well fitted to chronicle the annals of Tombstone's future progress, and protect—

CITY GOVERNMENT.

IN ITS city officials, Tombstone is peculiarly well represented, its personnel being composed of public-spirited citizens of intelligence, who occupy their official positions wholly to serve the better interests of the community that has become their pride through long association, and to conserve the better interests of the city with whom they have passed through a history-making epoch. Their tenure in office has been distinguished by honesty and dignity, and has added to the respect they have always borne as individual citizens. Their term will be memorable because of its being the one that granted to the El Paso & Southwestern Railroad the franchise that permitted the building of the railroad into this city.

The mayor, A. Wentworth, mention of whose long public career appears elsewhere in these pages, was elected to his present office last November, and may be trusted to fulfill the duties of his municipal trust with the ability that has distinguished his many years as a county officer.

ness man, prominent in fraternal circles, and an esteemed member of this community.

Mr. B. Hattich, who is serving his second term as city councilman for the second ward, is a representative citizen of long standing in this community; and is for the second time treasurer of the city of Tombstone, of whose pioneers he is also numbered. He is also a pioneer in the word's broader sense, having been a citizen of Colorado many years ago. He was the first supervisor of Hinsdale

GROUP OF TOMBSTONE RESIDENCES.

RESIDENCE OF T. R. BRANDT.	RESIDENCE OF M. C. BENTON.	RESIDENCE OF J. A. ROCKFELLOW.
RESIDENCE OF G. W. SWAIN.	RESIDENCE OF MRS. WM. RITCHIE.	RESIDENCE OF C. W. BLACKBURN.
	RESIDENCE OF SCOTT WHITE.	

The first ward is represented in the council by Joseph McPherson, who is now occupying the office of councilman for a second time. He is one of the city's foremost citizens, and makes a matter of personal concern everything that may tend towards forwarding the community's interest. He was elected supervisor of this county in 1896, and has been school trustee of this school district for three years. He was identified with its large freighting interests, and is at present proprietor of the McPherson transfer system. Mr. McPherson is fifty-two years old, is an energetic business man, prominent in fraternal circles, and an esteemed

county, to which office he was appointed by Governor Hill, before Colorado was yet a state. He was also commissioner of San Juan City, Colorado, where he still retains property interests. Mr. Hattich is sixty-five years of age, and is still hale and hearty. He is one of the oldest Knights of Pythias members in Arizona, and is one of the few upon whom the honor of a veteran jewel of that order has been conferred. He is married and has two children—Miss Rose Hattich and William Hattich, the latter at present publisher of the PROSPECTOR.

Councilman A. Ashman, of the city's third ward, was also a member of the council during the term preceding the present one. He is one of Tombstone's earlier pioneers, is a man of exemplary character, and, like his colleagues, enjoys the respect and trust of the entire community. Mr. Ashman is a native of London, England, and is sixty-one years old. He came to the United States in 1867, and entered Arizona one year later. He became a resident of Tombstone in 1879, and was employed at the vocation of mechanical engineer until 1894. He then purchased the gas plant of the Tombstone Gas Company, of which he retained active management until its recent acquirement by the Tombstone Improvement Company. He retains many other property interests in Tombstone and its vicinity.

The councilman from the fourth ward, Mr. William Cavanaugh, is a gentleman of quiet demeanor and worth, to whose care many public interests may safely be intrusted. He is now serving the second term in his present capacity, and is also clerk of the council. He is thirty-nine years old, and is a trusted employe of the Tranquility Mining Company, in whose service he has remained for several years. He is married and has three sons—William, Ernest and Clarence.

GEORGE BRAVIN.

GEORGE BRAVIN, Tombstone's chief of police, is not only socially qualified for his position by an intimacy with the city and its condition, obtained through long official service here, but he is deservedly popular with the whole community. His record as a public officer is above reproach, and his physical courage is a known quantity. He served as deputy sheriff under Sheriff Kelton, and occupied the position of undersheriff for two years under Sheriff Scott White. During his last term he was called on to face imminent death in the discharge of his duty, and that he did not falter was but fulfillment of his many friends' conviction. A notorious bad man of this region covered Bravin with a rifle and demanded the jail keys, that were in the officer's possession, but the latter, far from delivering the keys, seized the muzzle of the desperado's gun, and was shot during the struggle for its possession. That courageous act has made more respected the character of a man who always was held in high esteem by Tombstone's people. He was the first constable elected in the mining camp of Pearce. Mr. Bravin is a married man, and has five children—Etta, John, Lizzie, Valentine and Richard.

CHARLES BOWMAN.

CHARLES BOWMAN, city attorney, is one of Cochise county's leading lawyers. He is thoroughly grounded in the rudiments of his profession, and, although a young man, enjoys a lucrative practice. He is a member of the well-known firm of English & Bowman, of this city. He has been city attorney of the city of Tombstone for two years, and has given the city efficient service in that capacity. Formerly he was city attorney of the city of Tucson, where his administration was characterized by the same marked ability that has made his reputation as a lawyer of capacity in this county. Mr. Bowman is a staunch Republican, a gentleman of pleasing address, kindly and courteous of manner, and is one of Tombstone's most popular young men. He is thirty-three years of age, and is a native of North Carolina.

A. V. LEWIS, SHERIFF.

IN the wide scope of Western life there are few public offices that entail so much direct responsibility as that of sheriff. The incumbent, to successfully fulfil the requisitions of his position, must possess the mental ability of the man of affairs with the physical attributes of a frontiersman. Not only does his jurisdiction require an understanding of the technicalities of a varied clerical business and a working knowledge of the law, but he must often lead his deputies over waterless desert stretches and through almost inaccessible mountain ranges, on "man hunting" expeditions that require great physical endurance and indifference to personal danger. Cochise county is fortunate in possessing a man eminently fitted by physique and training to hold that arduous public office. Adelbert V. Lewis, the "big sheriff" of this county, has an enviable record as a peace officer. He was elected constable at Payson, Pinal

A. V. LEWIS.

county, in 1886, and gratified the men who had voted for him by his clean discharge of the official duties he had assumed. In Bisbee he was elected constable every time he was a candidate for that office, preserving the great Copper Camp's peace exceptionally well during three terms. The reason of "Del's" efficiency is his enormous physical strength and equable temper. He is a veritable son of Anak, towering more than six inches above a six-foot man's head, and is broad-shouldered in proportion; but he is genial, with a good nature and tolerance that characterize huge men. Mr. Lewis is as brave and honest as he is big, and has given Cochise county a most successful administration. He was elected to the office in 1900 by an unprecedented majority, and was re-elected to his present term with even a greater number of votes to spare. He married in August, 1892, a popular Bisbee young lady, Miss Lila Edwards, and has two children. His half tone is an excellent likeness of our big and popular sheriff.

GEO. B. WILCOX, CLERK DISTRICT COURT.

GEORGE B. WILCOX, clerk of the District Court of the county of Cochise, has a brilliant record as a soldier and stands high in the esteem of his fellow men because of an official and private life qualified by ability

GEORGE B. WILCOX.

and integrity. He came to Arizona in 1885 and enlisted with the famous old "I" troop of the hard-riding Fourth cavalry. That was during the campaign against crafty old Geronimo, when Uncle Sam's troopers had plenty of grim work cut out for them around the Mules, Dragoons and neighboring country. In consequence of qualifications of education and experience Trooper Wilcox was promoted to hospital steward, United States army, In 1890 he was appointed supervisor and steward of the Asylum for the Insane of Arizona and filled that position for two years with competence and distinction. When the United States called for volunteers to carry on the war with Spain, Mr. Wilcox enlisted, April 30, 1898, in troop B, First cavalry, United States volunteers, known throughout the world as Roosevelt's Rough Riders. Later, Mr. Wilcox became acting captain, commanding his troop from June 24, 1898, until his regiment was mustered out, September 15 of that year. He was elected justice of the peace of Bisbee in 1900, but resigned that position to assume his present duties as clerk of the District Court, to which position he was appointed April 1, 1901. Mr. Wilcox is a native of the city of Arrison, New York, and is thirty-nine years old. An excellent likeness appears herewith.

C. A. WALLACE, COUNTY SCHOOL SUPERINTENDENT.

CHARLES A. WALLACE, Cochise county's school superintendent, is a gentleman of exceptionally good standing in this community and is one of this city's pioneers, having passed his early school days in Tombstone. In its early days his father, one of Tombstone's most esteemed citizens of the past, served here as city recorder, and later in the capacity of county clerk. The subject of this sketch served ten years as deputy recorder of San

Diego county, California, where he went from Tombstone. Since returning to Cochise county he has been regarded as one of its most useful members. He was recently with the Copper Queen Company at Bisbee in the capacity of head timekeeper. He was elected county school superintendent in 1902. Mr. Wallace and his wife, who formerly was Miss Nellie Thieme, of Minneapolis, have one child, Charles, nine years old.

J. F. DUNCAN, CLERK BOARD OF SUPERVISORS.

J. F. DUNCAN, the present clerk of the board of supervisors of Cochise county, has been an active citizen of this vicinage for almost a quarter of a century, and has been identified with its public affairs almost continuously for that time. He came here in 1879, when what is now Cochise was still Pima county. He first settled in Bisbee, serving that community as its first justice of the peace. Subsequently, 1880-1882, he represented the new county in the territorial legislature, the Twelfth assembly. Since he became a resident of Tombstone he has filled many county and city offices with credit. He has been United States commissioner, court commissioner, and, during two terms, 1892-1896, was justice of the peace in this city. His entire service in that capacity in this county aggregates eleven years. He was also elected a member of the city council of Tombstone and served a term as city treasurer and city clerk. At the age of sixtyfour Mr. Duncan is still a hale man and an efficient public servitor, as may be attested by his long tenure in his present official position, which he has occupied continuously since 1898. It is a source of gratification alike to the individual and the community when a public official's capacity and faithfulness meet with steady recognition. It bespeaks

JAMES F. DUNCAN.

close attention to its people's interests on the part of its administration when they thus continue in encouragement of integrity and ability in the public's servitors. Mr. Duncan is a thorough Arizonan and has great faith in the future greatness of the treasure territory, and Tombstone in particular.

FRANK R. O'BRIEN, PROBATE JUDGE.

FRANK R. O'BRIEN, Cochise county's present probate judge, is a genial and vigorous citizen, with a wealth of experience in public affairs to season him for the brilliant political career his many friends predict for his

F. R. O'BRIEN.

future. His marked popularity was shown in the recent election, he being the only Republican on the county ticket chosen by the voters to serve them. Mr. O'Brien is thirty-eight years old and is a native of Vallejo, California. He occupied a position in the office of the city clerk of Oakland and was one of the military instructors at Whittier State School. He was military commandant at the California Military Academy, where he was also employed for some time as teacher. He was also identified with the California National Guard continuously for ten years. He attended the Law College of the University of California, which obviously increases his qualification for his present official position, in which the more abstruse points of law are so often involved. In Cochise county he has held several important positions with prominent business men— notably with Soto Brothers, of Willcox—and had charge of large commercial interests at Gleeson. He was the latter town's first postmaster, and held that position for three years, resigning when elected to his present office. His family consists of his wife and their eight-year-old daughter Gladys.

Mr. O'Brien's kindly disposition and spirit of accommodation is manifest in his courteous treatment of all those having dealings with him in his official as well as private capacity. His well known ability and the deep regard entertained for him by this county's voters make his future as a public officer assured.

Mr. O'Brien is a typical Westerner, with whom to have private or official business relations is an assurance of most cordial and courteous treatment.

SETH H. LEAVENWORTH, DISTRICT ATTORNEY.

SETH H. LEAVENWORTH is counted among the early Arizonans, having first visited Tombstone during her palmy-day experiences. He is an active practitioner of many years' Eastern experience and has gained a well merited reputation as an attorney of ability. Mr. Leavenworth was a member of the law firm of Leavenworth, Neale & Goodbody, of Bisbee, the partnership recently dissolving upon the election of Mr. Leavenworth to the office of district attorney of Cochise county. Prior to his location at Bisbee, Mr. Leavenworth was largely interested in a valuable mining venture in Mexico, the prosecution of development of which is now being conducted by an Eastern company, with which he is also identified. Mr. Leavenworth is careful, industrious and painstaking in his professional duties, and his uniformly courteous and pleasing manner has won for him the friendship, respect and admiration of the court, bar and the public. He assumed his duties as district attorney of Cochise county on January 1 of this year, having been elected at regular election two months prior. Mr. Leavenworth is a firm believer in the tenets of the Democratic faith and thinks Arizona's future is one of unparalleled prosperity in mining and commercial development.

L. HART.

THE competent assayer is one of the most important integers in the ensemble of any mining community. In fact, he is an absolute essential; a cog in the machinery of mining industry, without which movement could not exist. The thorough assayer has invariably become such through long and continued experience; for, although a knowledge of chemistry and metallurgy fits a man for the assayer's calling, it is only through long practice that he may become the infallible assayer who is such an invaluable factor in the progress of the modern mining world. Such an assayer is L. Hart, of this city. He came to Tombstone in 1879, from Nevada, with a wealth of mining experience gained in that section. When he first established his business here, this city was a rough, gun-fighting frontier mining camp of the most lurid type; and the reminiscenses Mr. Hart possesses of Tombstone's wild and wooly past would make a volume of absorbing interest. One of the famous feuds of this city's early days has left a lasting impression on his mind, the gun-fighters giving a very creditable performance with all kinds of real bullets within a few yards of his place of business. Mr. Hart still conducts an assaying business in the building in which he began nearly twenty years ago, and where he was for some time associated with F. C. Earle, now manager of the El Paso Smelting Company. One of the more important positions occupied by Mr. Hart in this region was charge of the assayer's department of the El Gachi Mining Company, of Sonora. He is sixty-six years old, and is one of the best known and most thoroughly competent assayers in the Southwest. He is one of the sturdy pioneers of Tombstone who have never faltered in their confidence in Tombstone's future.

RYBON & GEORGE.

THE Arizona Club, owned by Messrs. Rybon & George, is a first-class house, well conducted and up-to-date in every particular, and the brands of liquors and cigars carried by its bar are of an excellence that makes the club one of the most popular resorts in this section. Ben Rybon, who is fifty years old, came to Arizona eighteen years ago. He first became a resident of Prescott, where he followed mining, and was identified with the sheriff's office of Yavapai county. He is also interested in good mining properties in this district, is an experienced mining man, and expects extensive improvements in this mining zone in the near future. Richard George, although a young man, being thirty-six years of age, has been connected with prominent interests throughout the territory, and has been a railroad contractor and ditch builder in various parts of Arizona. The above-named gentlemen are well known in Tombstone, and enjoy a wide popularity with many residents of the city and its neighboring towns and country.

T. R. BRANDT.

T. R. BRANDT, cashier of the First National Bank of Tombstone, is essentially an Arizonan, and an old resident of Cochise county. Mr. Brandt was located at San Simon for many years, being a successful business man, and contributed largely to the material prosperity of his section in mining and cattle interests, with which he was also identified. Mr. Brandt, in common with all Tombstone residents, has great confidence in the future prosperity of this section, and has backed his judgment by substantial investment, and, besides his other interests, owns a most handsome residence, a half-tone production of which appears in these pages.

JAMES F. WALKER.

THE subject of this sketch, James F. Walker, came to Tombstone from Leadville in 1882, and was one of the first to preside over the destiny of the old Grand Central hoist. He has seen much experience as a mechanical engineer, and is regarded as a thorough and trustworthy exponent of that calling. In 1899 he entered his present business as a partner in the firm of Benton & Walker, but subsequently withdrew from that business and established his present place, the Capital, whose stock of liquors and cigars is one of the best. Mr. Walker has a large and varied experience in connection with mines, and his judgment has led him to become interested in local mining property, of which he has extensive holdings. The Walker group, a valuable group of mines in this district, are now being worked under bond by eastern capitalists. Mr. Walker is one of those men who have faith in indications of mineral in this district, which appeal to him, according to the past experience, so strongly as to lead him to believe that the unseen below the surface has in store mineral values that, if developed, will add to the world's wealth, and that he has been able to interest mining investors in his property, would seem to justify his judgment. He is forty years old, and was married in 1890 to Miss Margaret Kernan, of San Diego, California. They have four children—Frank, aged eleven; Rose, aged eight, and Dewey and Florence, four and two years old, respectively.

FLY'S PHOTOGRAPH GALLERY.

THE progress that has been made within recent years in the art of photography is nothing short of marvelous. The methods, apparatus and even manner of posing are virtually revolutionized in the march of progress. In no photographing establishment is this more strikingly illustrated than in the gallery of Mrs. C. S. Fly, of this city.

Mrs. Fly is acknowledged as one of the best artists in the photographic line in Arizona, and the years of establishment here have sustained the reputation. Besides finishing high class photo work, Mrs. Fly has negatives of some interesting views of historic interest in pioneer and Indian annals of Arizona's past, prominent among which are views of famous Apache chiefs and Indians taken at their native heath, while views associated with the pioneer mining history of Tombstone and Bisbee are to be obtained at reasonable rates.

JAMES REILLY.

AMONG the old pioneers whose careers have been closely interwoven with Arizona's upbuilding history is Judge James Reilly, of Tombstone, who has seen years of service within the border limits of the treasure territory, and besides attaining honor and prominence in the commonwealth he has helped to build, still enjoys the vigorous health which so well befits the dauntless spirit of the Arizona pioneer. Judge Reilly is recognized as one of Arizona's eminent attorneys, and has achieved great success in his profession. His large experience, sound judgment and acknowledged authority on mining law has won for him a proud distinction and enviable reputation. He successfully conducted many prominent and notable mining cases, unquestionably the most important in Arizona litigation, involving valuable property interests, and numbered among the most aggressively contested suits in her judicial history. While his professional work has necessarily occupied much of his time, he has not been blind to the duties imposed by good citizenship and has been elected to official positions on numerous occasions, serving his home county in legislative, county and city official capacities with capability, ever manifesting the keenest interest in the welfare of his section. Judge Reilly is one of Tombstone's respected pioneers, and besides property interests here, is interested in some valuable mining property in the county.

O. GIBSON.

O. GIBSON is a young man of sterling worth and a lawyer of ability. Although but thirty-two years of age, Mr. Gibson has, since being admitted to the bar in Arizona in 1895, demonstrated a natural proficiency and qualification that assures for him a bright professional future. Mr. Gibson first came to Arizona in 1883, locating at Flagstaff. He was for nearly sixteen years a resident of that section, and in 1898 moved to Cochise county, and after a stay of two years at Willcox in the practice of law, moved to Tombstone, forming a partnership with Judge James Robinson. The firm has since been dissolved, and Mr. Gibson, who is a ripe scholar, energetic, studious, of industrious habits and faithful to clients, accumulated a big share of clientage. He served as deputy district attorney during part of last term, and made an excellent record as public prosecutor. Mr. Gibson is also prominently identified with the work and labors of the Good Templars organization. He has devoted much time and accomplished much good in this field in Arizona, and his able lectures and forcible literary contributions are regarded as most effective arguments in the cause. He has served as grand chief templar of the Arizona jurisdiction for three years. In 1902 Mr. Gibson was candidate for delegate to Congress on the Prohibition ticket, and received a good complimentary vote by those who rallied to the standard of prohibition.

FRANK W. GOODBODY.

FRANK W. GOODBODY is not only a lawyer of recognized ability, but his genial nature and happy facility of expression make him a desirable addition to any community. He has not long been a resident of Tombstone, but his thorough knowledge of law and inherent talent have already secured for him an enviable reputation and a lucrative practice in this city. Mr. Goodbody is a native of Muskegan, Lake county, Illinois, where he was born January 28, 1865. He attended the law school of the Northwestern University, of Evanston, Illinois, graduating with a diploma of Bachelor of Law, and was admitted to the bar by the Supreme Court of that state. Later, he went to California and practiced his profession in several counties of the Golden State, and was for two years deputy district

equaled, have made him noted as a criminal pleader throughout the West. His ability has contributed largely to the outcome of many of the most celebrated law cases of this region's history, more notably in famous mining contests and prosecution of criminal cases that have formed some of the most noted law suits in the criminal annals of Arizona. Mr. English was born in Saginaw, Michigan, forty-three years ago, of Scotch-Irish parents. His father, who lived to the advanced age of eighty-eight years, was a prominent shipbuilder of that northern state, while his mother came of one of the first families of Maryland, the Fitzgeralds. Mr. English is essentially a pioneer of Tombstone, for, although he practiced law for a brief time in the city of his birth, he came to Tombstone in 1880, when he was twenty years of age. He was elected district attorney of Cochise county for three terms, first in 1887, but

FAMOUS ROSEBUSH AT THE C. W. BLACKBURN RESIDENCE.

attorney of San Diego county. He was also an ensign of the Naval battalion of the First division of the National Guard of California. He came to Arizona in 1901 and became a member of the law firm of Leavenworth, Neale & Goodbody, of Bisbee, but later the firm dissolved, and Mr. Goodbody established himself in Tombstone. He is now acting deputy district attorney for Cochise county, and has served one term as county school superintendent. He is an esteemed citizen of Tombstone, and a lawyer whose future is assured of large success.

ALLEN R. ENGLISH.

WHAT has been called the science of law has in Arizona no more brilliant exponent than Allen R. English. His forensic gifts, allied with a thorough knowledge of jurisprudence and mental resourcefulness, seldom

because of the large law business his ability has secured for him, he has not found it expedient to become a candidate for political honors since his last official service. Mr. English has become wealthy in consequence of his mining interests and professional practice. He owns valuable property in other portions of the territory, but continues to make his home in Tombstone—not only endeared to him by past associations, but pregnant in his belief with its resources that will make it once again known throughout the world on a grander scale than ever heretofore. A half-tone reproduction of the beautiful English residence in this city illustrates this sketch. His law office holds one of the most complete libraries in the West, containing several thousand volumes on law alone.

To keep posted on the mining development of Cochise county, subscribe for THE PROSPECTOR.

GEORGE W. SWAIN.

GEORGE W. SWAIN is one of the pioneer residents of Tombstone and enjoys a wide circle of acquaintanceship throughout the Southwest. Mr. Swain is a typical Westerner, having braved frontier life and vicissitudes since early manhood, the years of '61 and '62 finding him at the mining excitements of Nevada and California. For some years he was located in San Diego county, California, engaged in mining, and was one of the original discoverers of the famous Tom Scott mine, near St. Julian. The year 1880 marked his advent to Tombstone, since which time Mr. Swain has been honored with numerous elective positions of trust. In 1883 he was elected justice of the peace and the following year was city recorder of Tombstone. In 1888 Mr. Swain was elected city attorney, serving the term of two years with credit. As deputy district attorney for several terms Mr. Swain was recognized as a capable and efficient official, and in 1892 was elected public prosecutor

in Bedford, Ind., and attendance for almost three years at the law department of the University of Indiana. With the training of a symmetrical commercial and professional education acquired at special institutions, he is well qualified for an intelligent engagement in business pursuits and the successful conduct of private and public affairs. Mr. Woolery is twenty-six years old, an energetic scholar and attentive and observant of matters of legal import, which with experience will materially aid his steady advancement in the professional ranks. He was admitted to practice in Cochise county in January of this year, and is a rising young attorney, who is held in high regard by our citizens.

D. L. CUNNINGHAM.

ATTORNEY D. L. CUNNINGHAM, of this city, is a gentleman of professional capacity and a man of recognized integrity. Not only has he enjoyed the distinction of having the honorary degree of Doctor of Civil Laws conferred

RESIDENCE OF ALLEN R. ENGLISH.

of the county, overcoming a strong Democratic majority of that year. Matters relative to mining still possess a fascination for Mr. Swain, who owns a valuable group of copper properties in the Dragoon mountains, tributary to Tombstone. The property is regarded by mining men as a most promising one, and with development the realization of all that has been hoped for it is among the early probabilities. The Swain residence, on Fifth street, appears in reproduction elsewhere.

LEE O. WOOLERY.

LEE O. WOOLERY is a young man of sterling worth, who has before him a field of great promise, and in directing his attention to professional efforts as an exponent of the principles of Blackstone, has the advantage of good education, acquired in both public schools at his home

on him by Nashville College, Nashville, Tennessee, but he has established a reputation as a lawyer of ability throughout several states and the territory of Arizona. He was admitted to the practice of law in Alabama in 1887, in Flagstaff, Arizona, in 1899, and later was admitted to the bar of this territory by the Supreme Court of Arizona. He was also admitted to the bar in Colorado. He came to this city in November, 1902, and already has made his worth felt in this community, for although Mr. Cunningham is a young man, he is an earnest professional worker whose sincerity and ability have won for him the respect and confidence of all who know him. He is thirty-six years old, and though not a politician in the usual sense of the term, is an earnest advocate of Democratic principles, and has been an influential factor in the local ranks of that party during his residence in Arizona.

PITTSBURG-ARIZONA CO.

THE Pittsburg-Arizona Gold and Copper Company owns thirty mines—the largest group, excepting the Tombstone Consolidated Mines Company, in the Tombstone district. The company's officers are: H. T. Fisher, president; James McKay, vice-president; Edward H. Bindley, secretary-treasurer. Mr. Bindley is also assistant superintendent of the Pittsburg Steel Company, of Monessen, Pennsylvania, one of the largest of the world's great steel plants. Mr. McKay is a resident of Pittsburg, Pennsylvania. During the past two years they also have accomplished much development work in this district. In sinking, cross-cutting and levels they have done eight hundred feet of work.

On account of water near the surface, the mines had not been developed until they were acquired by Mr. Fisher, who organized the present company. They are now one hundred feet below the water level and have proven that the ore increases both in extent and value, and have two

the Mexican war, in the wanderings peculiar to his geological ilk, happened upon the outcroppings of the Bronco mine, which forms one of the Pittsburg-Arizona Gold and Copper Company's group. Attracted by the apparent value of the claim, he endeavored to develop it, but on account of its remoteness from civilization and the crude methods at the command of miners in those days, the professor had made but small headway in his work when the Apaches, after several bloody attempts, succeeded finally in wiping out of existence the German pioneer and his little force of miners. Several mounds show where the dead were buried after the several battles that were waged between the fierce aborigines and the courageous little band of pale faces. The Mexican inhabitants of that neighborhood long ago rumored that ghostly visitants had been seen about the adobe ruin in which Professor Bronco formerly had dwelt, and succeeding generations have enlarged upon the vague stories until at the present day there is firmly fixed in the sensorium of every Mexican in Charleston an unswerving

MILL OF THE PITTSBURG-ARIZONA MINING COMPANY.

carloads of ore ready for shipment. Formerly chloriders worked these properties above the water level, which is less than fifty feet below the surface, and shipped ore to the value of more than fifty thousand dollars.

The company also owns the Ground Hog mine, which is four hundred feet in depth, and was one of the steady producers in the early days of Tombstone. This property, the Tombstone and the Graveyard, now known as the Resurrection, were the first three mines located by Edward Schieffelin, who discovered and named the Tombstone district.

They have a ten-stamp mill, a picture of which appears with this article, two steam hoists, and will install a third by the first of April, on the double compartment shaft which they are now sinking. An air compressor is on the road which will furnish power for the drills used in sinking the same.

The mines have quite a romantic history. In the early sixties, Professor Bronco, a graduate of Freidburg University, Germany, a noted mineralogist and a veteran of

belief that every night during the dark of the moon a weird band of spooks arrayed in phosphorescent glow caper about in mad revel on the crumbling walls of the mouldering edifice. Since the present management has taken hold of the property, the old dwelling has been repaired and is now occupied by some of the men. Not long ago a superstitious miner erected a wooden cross, that no harm might be done to him. Many years after Professor Bronco's death, Captain Jeffords—Indian agent at Fort Bowie—and Mr. Delong made an attempt to work the mine, but they were forced to abandon the project because of the hostile Apaches.

A PROMISING GROUP.

AMONG the promising mining properties in the Tombstone district is the State of Maryland group, owned by Messrs. Fisher and Black. This group, which consists of five claims—Lucky Boy No. 1, Lucky Boy No. 2, Johannesburg, Montezuma and State of Maryland—is situated about two and one-half miles northwest of Tombstone, adjoining the celebrated State of Maine mine, which is fabulously rich in gold and silver.

Development work on this group on a large scale is contemplated in the near future. A shaft has been sunk on the Lucky Boy No. 1 to a depth of one hundred feet, and the ore taken out assayed upwards of several hundred dollars per ton. In the Johannesburg a tunnel has been driven to cross-cut the ledge. At a distance of five hundred and ten feet the formation has changed. Numerous veins and leaders have been uncovered which run from six dollars to twelve dollars in gold and from fifty dollars to two hundred dollars in silver. The Lucky Boy No. 2 has a tunnel of one hundred and forty-five feet, and is also very rich, both in gold and silver. This tunnel will be connected with a shaft of the Lucky Boy No.

the district and contiguous to the Emerald, the Comet and the Grand Central mines, controlled by the Consolidated Company. During a few years when the district was in its prime, these mines produced some half million dollars' worth of ore and were acknowledged as among the best in the district. They were worked at that time by the Watervale Mining Company, with headquarters in Chicago, which corporation extracted large bodies of ore of medium and high grade. In those days ore was shipped long distances at a great expense to the smelter, cutting down returns so that only ores of considerable value could be handled to a profit. The property is equipped with a fine hoisting plant, all enclosed, consisting of a fifty-horsepower Fraser-Chalmer double-cylinder engine, boiler house, work shops and office. The shaft is a splendid sample of timbering. It is a double compart-

BUNKER HILL M'G. CO.
INTERIOR VIEW of HOISTING WORKS.

1. The shaft on the Montezuma is now down eighty-five feet, and the ore from this place runs as high as that of the Lucky Boy No. 1. This shaft will be sunk to a depth of five hundred feet before any drifting is done. The State of Maryland, which gives its name to the group, has a shaft of ninety-five feet, and shows up very well. As Tombstone is rapidly regaining its former position, the above property is certain to come to the front.

THE BUNKER HILL MINING CO.

THE properties owned by this company are the famous Rattlesnake group of mines in the Tombstone district. They are three in number, are all patented claims and are known as the Bunker Hill, the Rattlesnake and the Mammoth. These claims cover an area of about sixty surface acres, are situated about two miles north of the city and, as shown by the map, are in the heart of

ment shaft, one for cage and the other for bucket. The condition of the shaft, owing to the dryness of the mine and its ventilation, is perfect. The facilities for handling the ores after extraction will be excellent, as the contemplated spur of the new railroad will go dirctly past the lines of the company. This fact alone will be of the greatest importance to the company, as ores can be shipped to smelters direct by cars. The ores in these mines occur largely in huge pockets, as is the case in most of the mines of this district. They consist of three principal varieties of ore. The first being of manganese dioxide carrying silver, forming the bulk of the medium and low grade deposits. The second being a carbonate ore carrying silver, lead, copper and gold. The third is in the form of an argentiferous galena carrying gold. Gold values are increasing with depth, as elsewhere in the camp, and all experts and mining men who have examined the property predict an increase in ore values as depth is attained. The shaft is now sunk to a depth of five hundred and sixty-five feet, with a winze of eighty feet below this. There are no signs whatever of water at this lowest working, and it is calculated that there are still some fifty or a hundred feet yet to be worked before the water level is reached. Drifts have been made by the old company at the two, three, four, five and five-sixty-five-foot levels, making at least a mile and a half of underground workings, including drifts and winzes. The Bunker Hill Mining Company of Tombstone is incorporated under the laws of Arizona. It is capitalized for a million shares at a par value of one dollar per share. On its board of directors are well-known men, and great success is predicted for the company. They propose to sink the main shaft at the earliest opportunity and ship ores to the nearest custom smelter. The officers of the company, all Tombstone residents, are C. R. Bostwick, ex-probate judge, president; E. W. Land, ex-district attorney, vice-president; Henry Wallace, M. D., secretary; P. B. Warnekros, merchant, treasurer; Stephen R. Hinkle, superintendent; Allen R. English, counsel; all well and favorably known Tombstonites.

INDEX